WOLFE TONE 225

EDITOR
Tommy Graham

COMMISSIONING EDITOR
Jim Smyth

PICTURE EDITOR
Sylvie Kleinman

PUBLISHING MANAGER
Nick Maxwell

DESIGN
Ger Garland

COPY-EDITING
Emer Condit

PRINTED IN IRELAND BY
W&G Baird Ltd

A *History Ireland* annual
FIRST PUBLISHED BY
WORDWELL LTD 2024,
Unit 9, 78 Furze Road, Sandyford
Industrial Estate, Dublin 18.
T. (+ 353 1) 2933568
F. (+ 353 1) 2939377
W. www.historyireland.com

ISBN 978-1-916742-11-6
First published 2024

All rights reserved. No part of this book may be reprinted or reproduced or utilised in any electronic, mechanical or other means, now known or hereafter invented, including photocopying and recording, or otherwise without either the prior written consent of the publishers or a licence permitting restricted copying in Ireland issued by the Irish Copyright Licensing Agency Ltd, 63 Patrick Street, Dún Laoghaire, Co. Dublin.

British Library Cataloguing-in-Publication Data. A catalogue record for this book is available from the British Library.

HISTORY IRELAND

Nine of the sixteen articles in this special supplement were delivered to a conference held in Clifton House, Belfast, and Dublin, in November 2023 to mark the 225th anniversary of the death of Theobald Wolfe Tone. (Search for 'Wolfe Tone 225' on YouTube.) And in Ireland—as both John Mulqueen's essay on left-wing republicanism and Guy Beiner's contribution on public memory so ably demonstrate—Wolfe Tone has always been with us. Marianne Elliott concluded her benchmark biography (1989) with a consideration of 'The Cult of Tone', whilst Christopher Woods in *Bodenstown revisited* (2018) showed how the annual 'pilgrimages' to Tone's graveside, with their attendant factional rivalries and shifting rhetorical projections, hold up a mirror to Irish political history more generally. Of course, Tone was only one among several of the 'founding fathers' of modern Irish republicanism. He owes his pre-eminence in the overcrowded pantheon of 1798 martyrs to the survival of his journals, published by his widow, Matilda, and his son, William, in Washington DC in 1826. Even so, observes Tom Bartlett, had his compelling writings been swept overboard on one of his always-perilous sea crossings, Tone would nevertheless have remained a historical figure to be reckoned with.

Why does Wolfe Tone still matter, and is there anything new left to say about him? The sheer variety of the essays in this supplement says aye to the latter question and witnesses to the complex and protean character of the man: Tone the Shakespearean, Tone the writer and clubman, and even, counterintuitively, Tone the republican, classical and emotive. Nor is there any need here for hagiography: Tone's human frailties were put on full display, and for all to see, by Tone himself. That humanity is epitomised by his encounter with Thomas Paine in Paris, recounted in these pages by Marion Kelly, when Paine attributed Edmund Burke's reported melancholy to the impact of his anti-Burkeian *Rights of man* (Burke's son Richard had recently died). Paine, commented Tone in his diary, had no children.

The past is unpredictable and every generation has something new to say about Martin Luther, Oliver Cromwell, Thomas Jefferson and Theobald Wolfe Tone. For instance, the advent of Matilda Tone as an exemplar of republican virtue—notably in the work of Nancy Curtin, and represented here by Catriona Kennedy's elegant essay—clearly reflects the salience of contemporary gender studies (although Mary McNeill wrote her biography of the republican, proto-feminist Mary Ann McCracken in the benighted patriarchal 1950s).

In the 1790s the original United Irish project was hobbled by sectarian frictions and crushed by massive State violence, and during the course of the nineteenth century Irish republicanism got entangled in, and almost submerged by, Catholic nationalism—'almost' only because of, as Louis Cullen observed, Fenian resistance to clerical *fiat*. 'Eternity is not long enough, nor hell hot enough to punish these miscreants', thundered Bishop Moriarty about the Fenians, who were certainly fighting a losing battle. In 1913 Patrick Pearse anointed Bodenstown 'the holiest place in Ireland'. In 1935 Aodh de Blácam nominated Tone 'one of the founders of modern Catholic Democracy'. Both statements are preposterous. In fact, as an ideologically sound republican, the author of *An argument on behalf of the Catholics of Ireland* and campaigner for Catholic relief from the penal laws was a convinced secularist.

A core principle of republican doctrine is the separation of Church and State. The American republic did not deny equal citizenship before the law to Catholics or Jews, just as the French republic likewise affirmed the equality of Protestants and Jews as citizens. Perhaps Tone's greatest legacy is that his aspiration 'to abolish the memory of all past dissension; and to substitute the common name of Irishmen in place of the denominations of Protestant, Catholic and Dissenter'—still unfinished business—laid down the template for a modern definition of Irishness, a nationality based on rights and on citizenship. In the face of a burgeoning narrow and hate-filled 'ethno-nationalism', both at home and abroad, his grave in Bodenstown is surely stirring. But as Tone himself was wont to say, '*Nil desperandum*'. He has bequeathed us the values—and humanity—to counter it.

TOMMY GRAHAM
JIM SMYTH

HISTORY IRELAND/ **1**

CONTENTS

4 Who or what was Theobald Wolfe Tone?
Thomas Bartlett

12 Wolfe Tone and the eighteenth-century republican ideal
Jim Smyth

17 Tone the polymath? His early Dublin club life
Martyn Powell

23 'The test of every man's political creed'—Wolfe Tone and the French Revolution
Ultán Gillen

29 Wolfe Tone's Belfast relationships and their influences
Kenneth L. Dawson

35 'Republicans and sinners'—Wolfe Tone and William Drennan
Fergus Whelan

39 How radical was Wolfe Tone?
Timothy Murtagh

44 Feelings and 'literary fame'? Tone's self-writings and the reader experience
Sylvie Kleinman

51 'All the world's a stage'—Theobald Wolfe Tone and Shakespeare
Eilís Smyth

56 Matilda Tone—'a worthy relict'
Catriona Kennedy

63 A meeting with Matilda—Thomas Cather's *Voyage to America*
Willa Murphy

66 Theobald Wolfe Tone Fitzgerald—1798 in 1916
Donal Fallon

71 'Breaking the connection with capitalism'—Wolfe Tone and the Irish republican left
John Mulqueen

76 Conor Cruise O'Brien's Tone—an exceptional case?
Marion Kelly

80 Writing *Wolfe Tone—prophet of Irish independence*
Marianne Elliott

86 Remembering the 'Father of Irish Republicanism'
Guy Beiner

92 Afterword
Bill Atkins

23 Tone was raised in a political culture heavily influenced by classical republicanism and that idealised the citizen-soldiers of the Irish Volunteers of 1778–82.

35 William Drennan—both he and Tone have a claim to be the leading writer in the United Irish cause.

WOLFE TONE 225

HISTORY IRELAND

www.historyireland.com

4

General Lazare Hoche, a long-time advocate of French intervention in Ireland, committed himself to Tone's invasion plan.

17

Tone in Volunteer uniform—the early years of his associational life, before revolutionary politics became all-encompassing.

51 Mrs Sarah Siddons appeared in Dublin in the same play in which Tone had acted at Galway in the preceding year.

56

The title-page of Rosamond Jacob's manuscript biography of Matilda Tone.

Mrs Margaret Tone with her sons Theobald (left) and Matthew (right). In his autobiography, written in Paris in 1796, Tone skips quickly over his childhood years. (Madden, *United Irishmen*/NLI)

BY **THOMAS BARTLETT**

WHO OR WHAT WAS THEOBALD WOLFE TONE?

THEOBALD WOLFE TONE was born in 1763: the year is significant (more on that later). In an autobiographical fragment written in Paris in 1796, at a time when he was 'about to embark in a business within a few days, the event of which is uncertain'—he meant nothing less than a descent on Ireland with a French fleet—he skips quickly over his childhood years, touches briefly on his time in Trinity College Dublin, and picks up the narrative in July 1785 with his courtship of Martha Witherington, aged fifteen, when to the fury of her family 'we ran off together and were married'. A child, Maria, quickly followed. Marriage had rendered Tone ineligible for a fellowship at Trinity, and he now decided on a legal career. He left (or abandoned) his wife and Maria to his family's protection and moved to London in early 1787 'to enrol as a student at law on the books of the Middle Temple'. Legal study bored him stiff, however, and his mind soon wandered—to the theatre, to schemes for a military colony in the Sandwich Islands (now Hawaii), plans for insurrection in the Spanish colonies in South America, to journalism, to co-writing a novel (*Belmont Castle*, published in 1790), 'to adventures with the fair sex', even to enlisting in the East India Company's army—in short, to anything but law. At length, having fulfilled his residence qualifications at the Middle Temple, Tone returned to Ireland in December 1788 and was called to the bar in July 1789. For a time he practised on the Leinster circuit but, as he recalled, 'I soon got sick and weary of the law' and, in any case, politics and pamphleteering beckoned.

Below: London's Middle Temple, where Tone enrolled as a law student in early 1787. Legal study bored him stiff, however, and his mind soon wandered.

THOMAS RUSSELL AND BELFAST

Tone published a pamphlet in defence of a new political association, the Whig Club, in 1790 but it had little impact; in his own words, it was 'barely above mediocrity, if it rose so high'. His next pamphlet was prompted by the threat of war

> '*What are the victories of Britain to us? Nothing! ... The name of Ireland is never heard, for England not our country we fight and we die.*'

between England and Spain in the summer of 1790. *Spanish war!* was an altogether more assured performance than the previous effort. In it, Tone dismissed any notion that Ireland had 'an obligation ... to follow Great Britain to war', and he ridiculed the idea that Ireland shared in British military triumphs: 'What are the victories of Britain to us? Nothing! ... The name of Ireland is never heard, for England not our country we fight and we die.'

It was also in 1790 that Tone encountered Thomas Russell and the two men quickly became firm friends. Russell was a half-pay army officer whose regiment was stationed in Belfast, a largely Presbyterian town with a population of about 18,000. Russell travelled north to join his regiment. It was to be a fateful move, for under the influence of the French Revolution Belfast was then seething with political unrest. Reformers there had failed in their attempts to secure reform of the Irish parliament in the mid-1780s, and now, inspired by events in France, were planning a new campaign with the same objective. However, the Catholic question—the admission of Irish Catholics to the political arena, the single issue on which previous reform movements had foundered—was still bitterly divisive. Russell, perhaps recalling some of Tone's views on this topic, asked his friend to suggest some appropriate resolutions for consideration at a Volunteer parade in Belfast on Bastille Day, 14 July 1791. On 9 July Tone replied, enclosing his resolutions, but he also privately declared as his 'unalterable opinion' that 'the bane of Irish prosperity is the influence of England', and that separation 'would be the regeneration of this country'.

AN ARGUMENT ON BEHALF OF THE CATHOLICS OF IRELAND

Tone's resolutions were essentially ignored, and by way of a riposte to this snub he resolved to become, as he put it, 'a red-hot Catholic', and he sat down to write what became probably the most famous pamphlet in Irish history: *An argument on behalf of the Catholics of Ireland*, published in August 1791. 'I am a protestant of the Church of Ireland, as by law established', he began, '... a mere lover of justice and a steady detester of tyranny', and then, his credentials established, he proceeded to point out forcefully to his readers that not only were Catholics capable of liberty but also there could be no liberty for anyone in Ireland until 'Irishmen of all denominations' united against the 'boobies and blockheads' that governed them and sought parliamentary reform. Tone's pamphlet had a great impact; within three months 6,000 copies had been sold and a further 10,000 were printed in 1792. Nevertheless, the work's novelty, as Tone's leading biographer, Marianne Elliott, notes, should not be exaggerated. The notion of a united front of all denominations in Ireland pursuing parliamentary reform had been the conventional wisdom in advanced reformist circles since the early 1780s. Still, it is fair to say that his *Argument* broke the log-jam holding up the development of a coherent reform strategy.

On the publication of this pamphlet, Tone was invited to Belfast to take part in the setting up of yet another new political club. He arrived there on 11 October 1791 in the company of Thomas Russell, who had earlier resigned his commission. Tone began to keep a diary

WHO OR WHAT WAS THEOBALD WOLFE TONE?

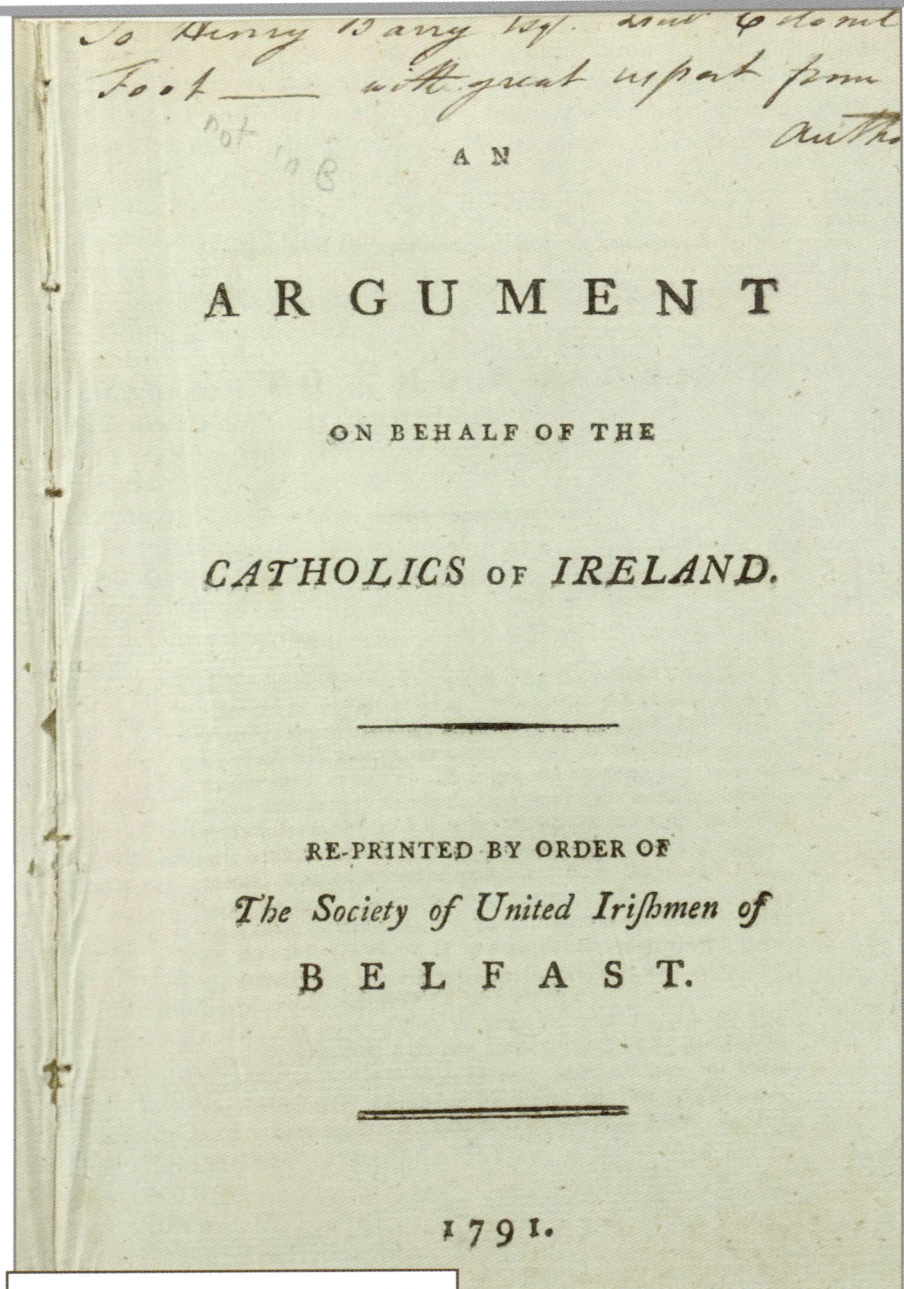

Above: A copy of *An argument on behalf of the Catholics of Ireland* (1791), inscribed by Tone, 'with great respect from the Author'. (Fonsie Mealy)

on his trip to Belfast, allegedly to keep his wife apprised of his activities there. From his journal entries of his stay, he and Russell appear to have spent most of their time drinking or recovering from the effects of over-indulgence. Such an impression is not altogether misleading: Tone was an intensely social being who loved conviviality and relished debate fuelled by alcohol, and Russell was a kindred spirit. There was, however, a serious side to all the dining, late nights and general junketing, for Tone was becoming acquainted with the advanced radicals of Belfast and, as the drink flowed, he was learning of the difficulties that lay in the way of fulfilling the aims of the new society. This society had been convened on 14 October and had held its inaugural meeting on 18 October 1791. Tone quickly established his authority over the proceedings, suggesting a new name for the society (preferring the 'United Irishmen' to the 'Brotherhood'), drawing up its resolutions (a tougher version of his July ones), and penning its declaration calling for 'AN EQUAL REPRESENTATION OF ALL THE PEOPLE IN PARLIAMENT'.

DUBLIN SOCIETY OF UNITED IRISHMEN

On 27 October 1791 Tone left Belfast and returned with Russell to Dublin, where they planned to set up a Dublin Society of United Irishmen. This was duly constituted on 9 November, but while Tone was active in its proceedings he was by no means the moving force. James Napper Tandy, a long-time radical in Dublin politics, took the lead, and he shared the running of the society with Dr William Drennan, whose pen now began to turn out a stream of publications propagating the cause of the United Irishmen. Tone became secretary to the Society, but this was a supporting role and he appears to have grown bored. All in all, after the heady days in Belfast, it was emphatically not the homecoming for which he had hoped. In addition, his finances were a pressing worry, for Matilda was expecting their third child, William, born in April 1792. Little money was coming in from Tone's legal work, and his (unsigned) contributions to the United Irish paper, the *Northern Star*, may not have been remunerated. Without doubt Tone was at a low ebb in his fortunes and prospects when in July 1792 he was appointed, in succession to Edmund Burke's son, Richard, assistant secretary to the Catholic Committee, with the handsome salary of £200 a year. Tone's writings had been well received by the more radical members of the Catholic Committee, principally John Keogh and Richard McCormick, and they could see positive advantages in having him as in effect secretary to their committee. By replacing Richard Burke with Tone, the Catholic Committee was clearly committing itself to a much more aggressive policy on political rights for Irish Catholics. Burke had, by and large, stood for maintenance of the existing order, hostility to any Catholic–Presbyterian alliance and hatred for the principles of the French

Revolution: it was notorious that Tone stood for the reverse of all these.

AGENT FOR THE CATHOLICS

The period from April 1792 to April 1793, when Tone was in fact agent for the Catholics, has a strong claim to being regarded as the happiest time of his life. He was active in organising the election of delegates to the Catholic Convention to be held in Dublin in 1792, and he was part of the delegation that went to London to lay their petition calling for political rights for Irish Catholics before King George III. Major concessions were duly delivered but Tone was not satisfied, dismissing the right to vote without the right to sit in parliament as 'partial and illusory'. When the Catholic Committee stood down, its job apparently done, Tone lost his job as secretary.

WAR WITH FRANCE AND THE JACKSON MISSION

At this time relations between Britain and revolutionary France were at breaking-point, and war was declared on 1 February 1793. With the outbreak of war with France, Dublin Castle instituted a crackdown on Irish reformers who had professed admiration for the French, and by the end of the year the United Irishmen and the reform movement were in disarray. Moreover, Tone's personal situation showed no signs of improvement. He had few legal briefs, and a new addition to his family (Frank, born in June 1793) added to the financial pressure he was under. Not surprisingly, he began to consider leaving Ireland and seeking his fortune elsewhere, possibly in the United States.

In April 1794 the Revd William Jackson, a Church of England clergyman of Irish parentage and a secret agent in the service of the French government, arrived in Dublin to sound out the prospects for a French invasion of Ireland. Tone met him and agreed to draw up a document outlining the likely reaction in Ireland to French descent on that country. Tone's report concluded that 'there seems little doubt but an invasion in sufficient force would be supported by the people'.

On 28 April 1794 Jackson was arrested at his lodgings on a charge of high treason, and his papers were seized. The case against him was a relatively strong one, for he had been under surveillance for some time and his letters had been intercepted. Tone was compromised and, to head off a prosecution, he entered into a compact with Dublin Castle that he would make a statement explaining his role in the Jackson affair, but he would not reveal confidences nor name names. In return, he would not stand trial and he would undertake to remove himself out of the kingdom to America. On 20 May 1795 Tone and his party, which included not only Matilda and the children but also his younger (and wayward) brother Arthur and his sister Mary, left Dublin for Belfast, whence they were to embark for America in some three weeks' time.

TO PARIS (VIA PHILADELPHIA)

Before Tone had left Dublin, he had held discussions with Thomas Addis Emmet and Russell, and had revealed his plan to make his sojourn in America a brief one and 'to set off

Below: Revd William Jackson, a secret agent in the service of the French government, who met Tone and other United Irishmen before his arrest in April 1794. (*Walker's Hibernian Magazine*, 1795)

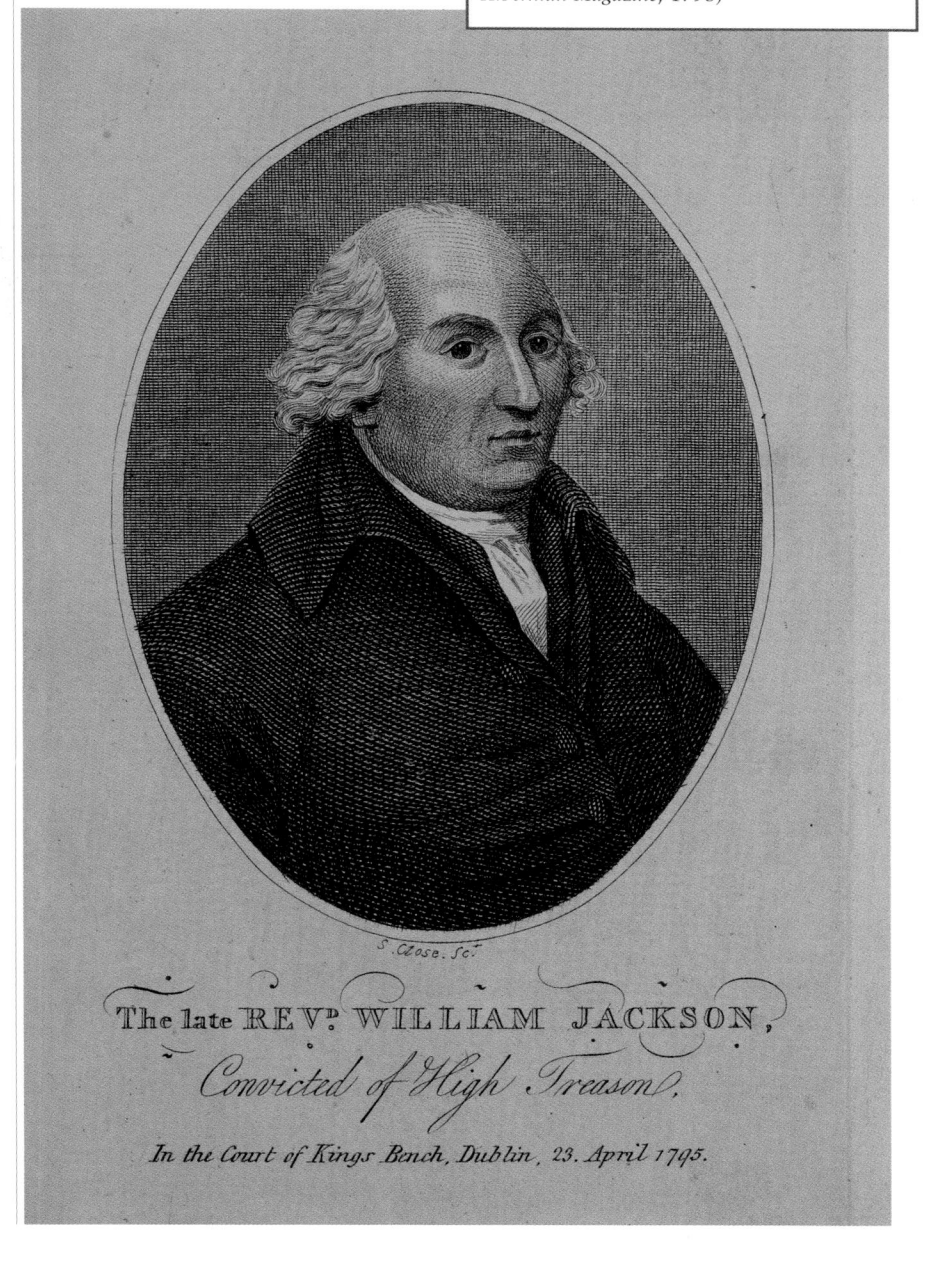

The late REV.^D WILLIAM JACKSON, Convicted of High Treason.

In the Court of Kings Bench, Dublin, 23. April 1795.

WHO OR WHAT WAS THEOBALD WOLFE TONE?

Above: James Monroe, American ambassador to France (and future president)—on his arrival in Paris on 15 February 1796, Tone presented Monroe with his credentials.

instantly for Paris and apply in the name of my country for the assistance of France to enable us to assert our independence'. He received significant support for this course of action from the Belfast radicals on his arrival in that town. Before he left Belfast, Tone and his friends visited McArt's Fort, high up on the Cave Hill, overlooking Belfast, and there they swore 'never to desist in our efforts until we had subverted the authority of England over our country and asserted her independence'. A day or two later, on 13 June 1795, the Tone party boarded the *Cincinnatus* and sailed for America.

As we shall see, Tone quickly came to hate America; he detested her politics and, as he saw it, Washington's craven subjection to British demands, and he pestered the French representative in Philadelphia, Pierre Adet, for a letter of introduction to the Directory in France. Once he obtained this, he set off (under the alias James Smith) for France, landing at Havre de Grace in February 1796—his mission: to persuade the French to launch an invasion of Ireland.

CITOYEN WOLFE TONE, *CHEF DE BRIGADE*

On his arrival in Paris (15 February 1796) Tone presented his credentials to the American ambassador (and future president) James Monroe, and then made his way to the French foreign ministry. He had an interview with the Irish-born French government official Nicholas Madgett, who was able to tell him that the French government, the Directory, was already seriously considering an expedition to Ireland. Tone wrote a memorandum calling for a force of 20,000 French troops, commanded by a leading French general, to be landed near Dublin. General Lazare Hoche, a long-time advocate of French intervention in Ireland, and Lazare Carnot, in charge of the Directory's war strategy, committed themselves to the plan. The Directory had been contemplating an attack on England and Tone's skilful advocacy would keep Ireland at the centre of French plans for the rest of the year. From March 1796 on Tone suffered disappointment and frustration as the project of an Irish expedition was beset with delays. Finally, on 16 December 1796, a French fleet crammed with 14,450 soldiers sailed from Brest. On board one of the sails of the line, the *Indomptable*, was 'Citoyen Wolfe

Below: General Lazare Hoche, a long-time advocate of French intervention in Ireland, committed himself to Tone's invasion plan.

Tone, *chef de brigade* in the service of the republic'.

The expedition may be accounted a complete failure. Encountering extremely severe winds and mountainous seas, the fleet was quickly scattered; while a number of ships reached Bantry Bay on 22 December, they were unable to disembark their soldiers, and in early January 1797 they limped back to Brest. For Tone, the months after the Bantry Bay expedition were a period of increasing frustration. He learnt of the Irish rebellion of May 1798 some three weeks after its outbreak, and it was not until September that he was able to take part in another, much smaller descent on Ireland. His ship was captured and Tone was taken ashore at Buncrana, Co. Donegal, on 31 October, where he was immediately spotted by Sir George Hill, a former classmate at Trinity and a noted loyalist in the north-west of Ireland. In irons, and under an escort of dragoons, Tone was conveyed to Dublin, where he was lodged in the Provost prison. A court martial soon followed, with sentence of death by hanging pronounced on him. As is well known, he cheated the hangman by inflicting a wound on his throat, which proved fatal. He was 35 years old.

To echo the words of Rudyard Kipling's boyish hero: 'I am a Sahib. No I am Kim. This is the great world, and I am only Kim. Who is Kim? Who is Kim—Kim—Kim? I am Kim. I am Kim. And what is Kim?' Who or what was Tone?

1763

The date of Tone's birth—1763—was significant. It marked the end of the Seven Years' War and the emergence of the British Empire, an empire on which famously the sun never set and which stretched from India to Canada, to the mainland colonies of North America, to the West Indies and back to London, Edinburgh and Dublin. Britain's extraordinary military successes, almost entirely at the expense of France, in India, the Ohio Valley, the West Indies and Canada profoundly destabilised the global order and set in train a series of events that led to revolutions—first in America, where Britain's attempts to recoup her financial expenditure brought push-back by the colonists and led seemingly inexorably to military conflict, revolution and independence; in France, where bankruptcy made necessary various unsuccessful financial remedies that ultimately brought about the calling of the Estates General and in short order, to use Edmund Burke's formulation, the revolution in France; and in Ireland, where, given the British government's need for vastly increased forces on land and sea, it compelled the Ascendancy to admit the majority Catholics into the 'circle of the constitution', a constitution hitherto strictly reserved for the minority Protestant élite. The resulting destabilisation of the Irish polity, a political order that had held firm since the 1690s, cleared the way for the rebellion of 1798. There were other revolutions as well, in St Domingo/Haiti, and clear signs of restlessness in Spain's South American possessions that eventually produced revolution in the 1820s. In short, Tone was born into, grew up in, sought to act a role in and tried to take advantage of the opportunities that offered in this new unstable, revolutionary world. That context, I think, explains one aspect of his career.

TONE'S MILITARY MEMORANDA

In the late 1780s Tone composed a number of memoranda detailing plans for a military colony in the Sandwich Islands, present-day Hawaii. This colony, garrisoned by some 500 soldiers, all 'under 30 years old', would be a base from which to plunder and invade—in the spirit of the 'Buccaneers who were my heroes'—Spanish possessions in South America. His proposal was hand-delivered to Downing Street, where it was ignored. Nothing daunted, Tone prepared a second 'enlarged and corrected' proposal in which he called for British support for the Spanish colonies to attain their independence. This too was politely dismissed. Finally, in 1790 Tone submitted yet another revised proposal, this one advocating what was nothing less than the eighteenth-century equivalent of the nuclear option. Yes, he would bring independence to the Spanish colonies but this time he proposed to ignite 'a great revolution, a revolution extending the blessings of liberty to the millions of slaves' in that region. Not surprisingly, for the liberation of slaves was no part of British government policy, this proposal was left to gather dust in the archives of the British Foreign Office. Six years later, by now a *chef de brigade* in France's army destined to invade Ireland, Tone mused on how British ministers William Pitt and Lord Grenville might regret that they had not taken up his offer of military service in the South Seas. By 1790, as well, Tone had tried 'twice or thrice' to enlist in the East India Company army—his brother William already served in it—but he had no success: he appears literally to have missed the boat.

This did not, however, end Tone's determination on military service abroad. The months of inaction that followed the failure at Bantry Bay saw him resigning himself to serving anywhere with the French army. In 1798 the rumour of a French expedition to India via Egypt stirred him to put his name forward for a command: 'I would I had a good map of Asia to see how far it is from Jerusalem to Madras', he noted, 'for I have a great eye on the Carnatic'.

From this brief resumé of Tone's plans for overseas adventures—and they must be seen as integral to his attempts at autobiography—it will be noted that his gaze is almost always fixed on the horizon, on faraway countries, on the South Atlantic, the Pacific, the Carnatic, on Paris, on anywhere but Ireland itself. It is significant that Tone himself at various times, for example in Bantry Bay while awaiting in vain to disembark as part of a French invasion force, wrote that he was not at all 'violently affected' by the sight of the land of Ireland, but 'look on it as if it were the coast of Japan'. And when Tone contemplated what would become of him after the 'great victory' in Ireland, he confessed that his ambition was to become not the president of Ireland but rather the first Irish ambassador to France, an office which would of course mean leaving Ireland and living in Paris. For Tone an added inducement for this post was that it came with a plentiful supply of 'diplomatic burgundy'.

> '... he confessed that his ambition was to become not the president of Ireland but rather the first Irish ambassador to France.'

THE FINEST DIARIES WRITTEN BY ANY IRISHMAN

During 1796–7, when he was not composing memoranda on the situation in Ireland and urging the French to speed up their preparations for invasion, Tone haunted the opera and many other theatres in Paris. Among the many performances he attended was 'L'offrande à la liberté', which he pronounced to be 'superb', and then explained that 'whenever the word "*esclavage*" [slavery] was sung it operated like an electric shock on the audience', and at the words '*aux armes citoyens*' in *La Marseillaise* 'all the performers drew their swords and the females turned to them as encouraging them'. On a second rendering of *La Marseillaise* 'around one hundred members of the National Guard rushed on to the stage with bayonets fixed, sabres drawn and the tricolour flag flying'. 'It would be impossible to describe the effect of this', Tone wrote, 'I never knew what enthusiasm was before.'

Nevertheless, Tone's diaries for his time in Paris in 1796 and 1797 also reveal his impatience, dismay and depression at the delays that dogged his mission. Equally, they show his fondness for irony and self-mockery, his impatience with anything that looks like humbug or pretentiousness, and a sense of fun and gaiety that has endeared him to readers ever since. They also speak eloquently to Tone's personality: in his diaries, probably the finest written by any Irishman, he charts his feelings as he deals with the various setbacks and minor triumphs that beset his quest. Such writings proved inspirational to later Irish revolutionaries—Thomas Davis, John Mitchel, Patrick Pearse and James Connolly among others. Taken together, Tone's writings make an important contribution to the literature of travel and to the literature of exile, and because they were written at the time they have an immediacy, a poignant immediacy, that is not to be found in the subsequent retrospective memoirs of other participants in the revolutionary 1790s or, indeed, later. The reader knows what the outcome of Tone's odyssey would be; Tone did not.

TONE'S LITERARY REMAINS

In 1797, in an interview with General Hoche, Tone was asked what form of government he could suggest for Ireland after English rule had ceased. Tone did not hesitate: 'Undoubtedly a republic', he replied. Later sympathetic commentators seized on this. 'If Tone did not, in his lifetime, achieve greatly', remarks Seán O'Faolain, 'he started much. Without him, republicanism in Ireland would virtually have no tradition.' There is much in this, but care is needed. The reality was, as Jim Smyth points out, that there was at that time no agreed definition of what constituted a republic or even a republican form of government. In May 1791 Dr William Drennan, a long-standing reformer and later founding member of the United Irishmen, had called for a new society to be set up with, as 'its general end, real independence to Ireland, and republicanism its particular purpose'. What Drennan meant by this was that in his republic the 'many', not the 'few', would have the greater power through a reform of parliament. His essentially civic republicanism would promote reforms in education, public health and the treatment of poverty, but crucially the connection with Britain would remain. For Tone it was all rather different. From an early date he was a republican separatist, believing that republicanism could not thrive in Ireland while the connection with Britain remained. The ideal of republican separatism was Tone's major contribution to the political history of Ireland.

In large measure, the republican tradition to which O'Faolain alludes was based on the publication in 1826 of Tone's literary remains—his journals or diaries, an autobiographical memoir, some letters and most of his public writings. The sheer mass, however, of Tone's published material—some 1,500 pages in two volumes—poses a problem for the historian. Can these weighty tomes be taken as an unequivocal endorsement of Tone's importance in the 1790s? The answer is, I think, yes: apart from the materials produced by Tone himself, there is the evidence from Irish manuscript repositories and, crucially, there is a mass of documentation in the French archives, all of which testify to Tone's importance to French plans. And, of course, *chef de brigade* commissions were not handed out to foreigners by the French military command without rigorous scrutiny.

WILLIAM TONE'S 'LIBERTIES'

Nevertheless, there is still a problem with Tone's writings as compiled and published by his son, William, with undoubted assistance or advice from his mother, Matilda. William declared that the 'only liberties' he had taken with Tone's writings were to excise or sanitise some cutting remarks by Tone on various members of the Witherington family, but he did much more than that. The fact was that Tone was nothing if not pass-remarkable—on women ('ugly', 'villainous ugly') and on the typical Englishman's neglect of his wife, 'which I did not fail to profit from', and he was especially scathing on America and Americans. In contrast to his love for all things French, including cuisine, landscape, martial spirit, military spectacle, opera, ballet and theatre, Tone had quickly come to detest everything about America, viewing 'with contempt and indig-

Above: William Tone—produced a sanitised version of his father's writings in 1826. (Madden, *United Irishmen*/NLI)

nation' its politics, its climate and its people (dismissed as boors). He obsessed over the prospect that if he remained there his daughter Maria might become the wife of an American 'clown without delicacy or refinement'. Clearly, William Tone could not allow such comments by his father to see the light of day, if only on grounds of prudence, for very many United Irishmen had controversially found refuge in the United States after the failure of the 1798 rebellion. There was enough anti-Irish feeling in America without adding to it.

Moreover, from the scattered references by Tone to his fellow countrymen it was obvious that, while he might have turned his back on the Ascendancy, he had not rejected the outlook of the Ascendancy. Priests, he declared, 'especially Irish priests, were very bigoted and very ignorant, slaves to Rome of course', and equally 'enemies of the French Revolution' which had rescued France from 'the yoke of popery and despots'. These remarks were cut from the published edition, yet Tone's ideas on getting Irish prisoners of war to enlist in French service were allowed to stand. He had earlier dismissed any such plan as 'nonsense', even 'flat nonsense', but he eventually came around to the idea. 'I know the Irish a little', he announced grandly, declaring that, since 'poor Pat is a little given to drink', the best way to get the POWs to enlist would be to march them to a port of embarkation under false pretences, 'send in a large quantity of wine and brandy, a fiddle, and some French *filles* [*de joie*]' and then, when 'Pat's heart is a little soft with love and wine', persuade them to 'take a trip once more to Ireland'.

Finally, any of Tone's remarks that might have suggested that he was flippant, frivolous or inconstant were carefully weeded out from the published volumes. A stray—and, be it said, innocent—remark that in Paris there were '*filles de joie sans nombre*' was cut. Moreover, the innocuous (and accurate) statement by Tone that his writings lacked 'system' was omitted, as were all references to the Tone family's 'romantic spirit of adventure'. In short, Tone cannot be pigeon-holed as simply an adventurer, a romantic or a revolutionary, though from the evidence of his writings he can be considered as a buccaneer for his military plans, a Boswell for his journals, a Byron for his dreams and a Mitchel for his republican separatism. Therein lies his charm and fascination.

- *Thomas Bartlett is Emeritus Professor of Irish History at the University of Aberdeen.*

FURTHER READING

M. Elliott, *Wolfe Tone, prophet of Irish independence* (2nd edn) (Liverpool, 2012).

S. Kleinman, '"*Un Brave de plus*": Theobald Wolfe Tone, alias Adjutant-general James Smith: French officer and Irish patriot adventurer', in N. Genet-Rouffiac & D. Murphy (eds), *Franco-Irish military connections, 1590–1945* (Dublin, 2009).

R.R. Madden, *The United Irishmen, their lives and times* (7 vols) (1842–60).

T.W. Moody, R.B. McDowell & C.J. Woods (eds), *The writings of Theobald Wolfe Tone* (3 vols) (Oxford, 1998–2008).

J. Smyth, *The men of no property* (London, 1998).

WOLFE TONE
AND THE EIGHTEENTH-CENTURY REPUBLICAN IDEAL

BY JIM SMYTH

WOLFE TONE'S REPUTATION in popular tradition as 'the founding father of Irish republicanism' is secure. It is also inaccurate. In the first place, there are a number of other candidates, such as William Drennan and Samuel Nielson, with equal or arguably stronger claims on that title. Secondly, republican ideas featured in Irish political discourse long before Tone, Drennan or Neilson were born. Tone may therefore be described more accurately as *one of* the founding fathers of *modern* Irish republicanism. Modern republican theory was forged in the crucible of the American and French revolutions, which some historians see as the two most powerful expressions of a late eighteenth-century Atlantic or democratic revolution, in which the United Irish movement of the 1790s took part. Yet while the republican principles of Tone and the United Irishmen were undoubtedly inspired by the American Declaration

> **'Real Whigs constituted a small minority coterie who achieved an ideological impact, left a deep historical imprint and generally boxed well above their contemporary political weight.'**

of Independence, the Fall of the Bastille and the writings of Thomas Paine, they also drew on an older 'commonwealth' or 'classical republican' inheritance.

'REAL WHIGS'

The Eighteenth-Century Commonwealthmen, more usually self-identified as 'Real Whigs', constituted a small minority coterie who achieved an ideological impact, left a deep historical imprint and generally boxed well above their contemporary political weight. The name denotes their adherence to the ideal of the English commonwealth, free state or republic, of the early 1650s, and two of the most crucial exponents of that ideal were Irishmen, John Toland and Robert Molesworth. Toland, by origin an Irish-speaking Catholic from Inishowen, Co. Donegal, converted to Protestantism as a teenager, and in 1688 as a student in Glasgow University he joined in the Presbyterian 'rabbling' during the 'Glorious Revolution' which overthrew King James's government in Scotland. Often cast as a mercurial political shapeshifter, Toland in fact never wavered in his commitment to the Williamite settlement. Best known for his free-thinking tract *Christianity not mysterious* (1697), in an astonishing burst of publishing productivity between 1698 and 1700 he turned out a sequence of classic English republican texts written by Edmund Ludlow, John Milton, Algernon Sidney and James Harrington. Almost single-handedly he had thereby created the literary canon of the Eighteenth-Century Commonwealthmen.

Robert, 1st Viscount Molesworth, was one of Toland's patrons. The term 'Anglo-Irish' has always been problematic, but if ever fit for purpose it does apply to Molesworth, who sat in both the College Green and Westminster parliaments and presided alternately over his landed estates in Yorkshire and Swords, north County Dublin. Molesworth's preface to *Franco-Gallica* (1721) was republished in 1775 as a free-standing pamphlet, *The principles of a real Whig*, and attests to the author's credentials as, in one critic's words, 'a snarling republican'. Molesworth's political and intellectual connections extended across England, Scotland and Ireland. English Whigs, after all, spoke in a political language common to Irish Protestant patriots and American colonists, albeit in local dialect, and, more broadly,

Above and opposite page: John Toland—best known for his free-thinking tract *Christianity not mysterious* (1697), between 1698 and 1700 he published a sequence of classic English republican texts by Edmund Ludlow, John Milton, Algernon Sidney and James Harrington, creating the literary canon of the Eighteenth-Century Commonwealthmen. Robert, 1st Viscount Molesworth (opposite page), was one of Toland's patrons. (Alamy)

shared in a common Anglophone literary culture—a culture steeped in emulation of classical antiquity.

CLASSICAL ANTIQUITY
The standards of literary excellence in Molesworth's time were 'Augustan' (alluding to the poets Virgil, Horace and Ovid, not the emperor). As a student in Trinity College in the early 1780s, Tone walked daily past the splendid Palladian edifice of the Irish parliament in College Green before entering through the gates of the university's equally pleasing neo-classical (or 'Georgian') west façade. Tom Bartlett observes that Tone's lifespan (1763–98) fixes him firmly, from first to last, as a man of the eighteenth century, and as such he benefited from a classical education. For example, Cicero's *De officiis* was a prescribed text on the college syllabus. Along with logic, ethics and natural philosophy, Tone studied Greek and, like every other student, sat a final *viva voce* examination conducted in Latin. Classical reference came easily to the classically literate upper echelons of eighteenth-century society. In 1795 Tone sailed into American political exile aboard the *Cincinnatus*, named after the renowned Roman statesman who, after serving his country, relinquished office voluntarily and 'returned to the plough'. A few months later, Tone's old ally in the Catholic Committee, John Keogh, wrote to him in New Jersey, wondering whether the London-trained, Dublin-born-and-raised barrister might also consider 'returning' to the plough. Keogh did not need to explain the allusion.

WOLFE TONE AND THE EIGHTEENTH-CENTURY REPUBLICAN IDEAL

Above: As a student in Trinity College in the early 1780s, Tone walked daily past the splendid Palladian edifice of the Irish parliament in College Green before entering through the gates of the university's equally pleasing neo-classical west façade. (James Malton, *A picturesque and descriptive view of the city of Dublin* (1791))

Nevertheless, for all that, in his writings, which are awash in literary quotation, Tone cites classical authors—Cicero and Virgil—only two or three times. Even more strikingly, he is silent on Locke, Montesquieu, Thomas Paine and many other obvious candidates from the Enlightenment repertoire—and he had certainly read both Locke and Paine. The absences are instructive. Tone had a literary imagination. He referred typically to the Swift of *Gulliver's travels*, not to the Swift of the politically overt *Drapier's letters*. Indeed, most of his literary allusions drew on eighteenth-century drama and, by a wide margin, on Shakespeare. That habit of mind can only cause headache for the historian of political thought. It does, however, call attention to the under-appreciated importance of theatre in the diffusion of political ideas.

SUBVERSIVE THEATRE

Clearly wary of the politically subversive potential of drama, on stage and in print, the Walpole administration stepped up official censorship with the introduction of the licensing act of 1737. The first play to be banned under the new law two years later was *Gustavus Vasa, the deliverer of his country*, a transparent political allegory attacking Walpolean corruption, written by an Irishman in London, Henry Brooke. As with copyright, however, British legislation did not extend to Ireland (unless Ireland was so named in the act), and so in 1744 the Smock Ally theatre in Dublin presented a performance of Brooke's play, retitled *The Patriot*. The ideological content of *The Patriot* aside, the mere act of performing it asserted Irish legislative independence, and, lest anyone in the audience miss the point, the stage curtains were embossed with an image of the College Green parliament. Three years later, the potency of theatre as a site of political contestation was again demonstrated by the Smock Ally, or Kelly, riot.

CATO, A TRAGEDY

Probably the most politically influential play in the eighteenth-century Anglosphere (comprising Britain, Protestant Ireland and the American colonies) was Joseph Addison's *Cato, a tragedy* (1712). Robert Harley, earl of Oxford, effectively the prime minister (the title and office did not yet exist), and the philosopher and future bishop George Berkeley attended the opening night in London, as did Sir Constantine Phipps, lord chancellor of Ireland, a few months later when the play came to Dublin. All three were Tories, which belies *Cato*'s stoutly Whig reputation and suggests that the politics of Addison's play are more complex, ambivalent or enigmatic than that reputation allows. Its popularity, however, is unqualified. Dublin editions were printed in 1730, 1732, 1746, 1749, 1750 and 1752, along with a Cork edition in c. 1767 and a Belfast one in 1772. Among the many London editions, that of 1764 is worth mention, if only because its gloriously prim title is too good to pass over: *Cato, a tragedy: by Mr Addison without the love scenes*.

Addison presented an Augustan fiction about the historical Roman senator Marcus Porcius Cato, also known as Cato the Younger, one of the leaders of the forces that opposed Julius Caesar when he 'crossed the Rubicon', launching a civil war that collapsed the republic and established an empire. And rather than submit to the victorious Caesar's somewhat generous peace terms Cato committed suicide. Tories like Berkeley and Phipps who applauded Addison's celebration of liberty chose to ignore his vindication of republicanism. But 'Real Whigs' of the commonwealth persuasion got the message loud and clear—as they read it, anyway. Beginning in late 1721, two Whig journalists, Thomas Gorden and John Trenchard, wrote a series of articles in the London press excoriating the wholesale corruption and reckless speculation of the political establishment in the South Sea Bubble scandal, subsequently published in pamphlet form as *Cato's letters*. In his *Ideological origins of the American Revolution*, Bernard Bailyn peerlessly captured that synergy of play and pamphlet:

> 'So popular and influential had *Cato's Letters* become in the colonies within a decade and a half of their first appearance, so packed with ideological meaning, that, reinforced by Addison's universally popular play *Cato* and the colonists' selectively Whiggish reading of Roman historians, it gave rise to what might be called a "Catonic" image, central to the political theory of the time, in which the career of the half-mythological Roman and the words of the two London journalists merged indistinguishably. Everyone who read the *Boston Gazette* of April 26, 1756, understood the double reference, bibliographical and historical, that was intended, by an anonymous writer who concluded an address to the people of Massachusetts as he put it without further explanation—"in the words of Cato to the free holders of Great Britain".'

Cato was General George Washington's favourite play and in the bitter winter of 1777–8 he had it performed before his beleaguered troops in the Congressional Army, encamped at Valley Forge. In 1776, when Nathan Hale, hanged by the British in New York City as a spy, famously proclaimed from the gallows 'I regret that I have but one life to lose for my country', he paraphrased *Cato*, 'what pity is it / That we can die but once to serve our country'. In 1795 Revd William Jackson, another eighteenth-century patriot who 'died for his country', charged with treason, poisoned himself in the Dublin high court dock. His last words to his attorney were 'we have deceived the senate'—a direct quotation from Thomas Otway's much-performed and much-reprinted play *Venice preserv'd* (1682). What ties *Venice preserv'd* and *Cato* together is the imaginative concept of Stoic, for which read republican, suicide.

DYING WELL
Tone read and almost certainly knew both plays as a theatre-goer, but, as in his refractory and elusive engagement with the canon of political theory, so in the matter of the influence of literature in shaping his political ideas he left little to nothing textually for the historian to work with. Tone quotes from both plays in his journals. And what does he reveal? Well, from *Cato*, 'I am puzzled in the mazes and perplexed by errors', and from *Venice preserv'd*, 'Hurry, durry, Nicky Nacky'—which from the context probably means something like 'time to get going'—but, in either case, there is not much ideological red meat for the historian of political thought to chew on. In *Antony and Cleopatra* Shakespeare invokes the Stoic virtue of honourable suicide: 'what's brave, what's noble, let's do it after the high Roman fashion, and make death proud'. Yet, true to form, Tone, who cites almost all of Shakespeare's plays, including two of the four Roman plays, *Julius Caesar* and *Coriolanus*, does not quote from *Antony and Cleopatra*. Shakespeare aside, however, Tone and his cohort did have much to say about dying well.

Reacting to reports in 1793 of a renegade French general's last moments on the guillotine block, Tone's great friend Thomas Russell records: 'hear of Custine's being executed and his terrors. Much sho[c]ked at it. I thought he would suffer but his irresolution is strange. A man who braved death in the field to be so timid on the scaffold … I am continually more affected than by anything I have long heard. Such inconsistency!' Once they had committed to armed insurrection, Russell and his comrades lived constantly, and consciously, in the shadow of death. 'Whether we fail or succeed', remarked Henry Joy McCracken, 'we expect to be the first to fall.' At the end on 17 July 1798 in Cornmarket Square in Belfast, McCracken, in the words of his former prison cellmate Charles Hamilton Teeling, 'evinced the firmness' on the scaffold 'which he had displayed in the field' at the Battle of Antrim. Tone was cut from the same eighteenth-century republican cloth. 'If I become not the gallows as well as another', he confided to his journals, then 'a plague on my growing up.'

'HE DIED LIKE A ROMAN OR SHOULD I SAY A FRENCHMAN'
On 31 October 1798, the Royal

Below: Joseph Addison's *Cato, a tragedy* (1712)—probably the most politically influential play in the eighteenth-century Anglosphere.

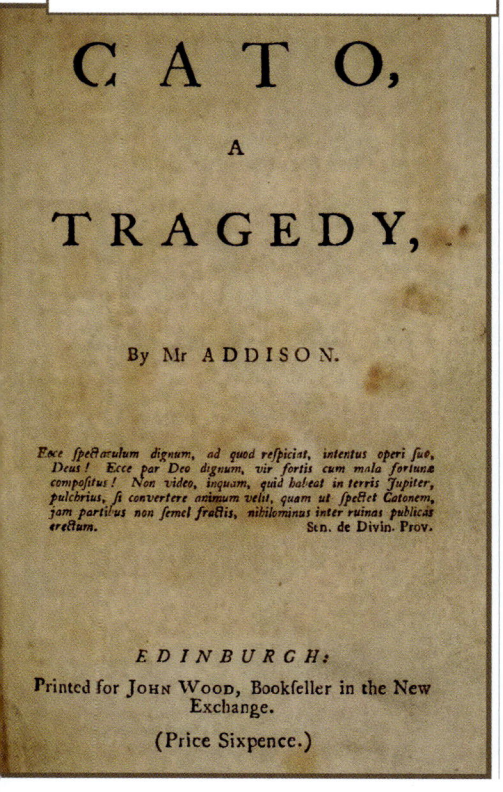

Navy intercepted and engaged a French flotilla near Lough Swilley, Co. Donegal. Tone, aboard the flagship, the *Hoche*, was observed to have fought 'with the utmost desperation, as if he were courting death'. Taken prisoner at Buncrana, he was soon recognised by a local magistrate, Sir George Hill. The two men had known each other since their Trinity College days and Hill wrote to Dublin Castle that Tone—his fate by then beyond all doubt—addressed him 'with as much *sang froid* as you might expect'. Clapped in irons and escorted by Lord Cavan and a troop of dragoons, the prisoner was dispatched to Dublin and committed to the Provost's prison to await trial for treason, by court martial. Tone, dressed in the uniform of an adjutant general, in possession of his commissions, and declared by his commander, General Hardy, to be a French citizen, protested 'the indignity intended against the honour of the French army in my person' and demanded his right to be treated as a prisoner of war.

The State, of course, proceeded to treat him as a natural-born subject of the Crown and a traitor. Sentenced to death, Tone chose to slit his own throat rather than collude in the dishonouring of his uniform and commissions by hanging. Prison cell suicides are by definition suspicious, and high-profile suicides such as Tone's invite speculation and invariably attract conspiracy theories; yet in the circumstances, and in accordance with the classical republican ethos, Tone's decision to take his own life by his own hand should hardly come as a surprise. It is said of Cato that whenever he is depicted in art it is always in the act of stabbing himself, and in addition Tone had several contemporary republican suicides and attempted suicides to contemplate. In May 1797 the French revolutionary Gracchus Babeuf tried but failed to kill himself in an effort to cheat the guillotine; three years earlier in Dublin Revd William Jackson, as we have seen, succeeded in thwarting the State. Tone later commented that Jackson's 'fortitude in a voluntary death must command the respect of the most virulent persecutor', while his fellow United Irishman William Drennan said that 'he died like a Roman or should I say a Frenchman'.

Cato killed himself rather than live under tyranny; if Jackson had been executed, his property would have been forfeit and his widow left destitute. In Paris in 1795 six condemned Jacobins committed suicide, asserting their personal agency and defying a Thermidorian regime which had betrayed the republic. All those 'voluntary deaths' conformed to Stoic doctrine on suicide, as did Tone's last, initially botched, supremely political act. Fatally wounded, Tone lingered on in agony for a few more days. Sir George Hill fumed that he 'would have sewed up his neck and finished the business', and Lord Cavan's fond 'hope' that the hanging of so notorious a rebel would 'amuse Dublin' was dashed, for Tone had other ideas, 'after the high Roman fashion'.

> **'Sentenced to death, Tone chose to slit his own throat rather than collude in the dishonouring of his uniform and commissions by hanging.'**

Below: *Cato's suicide* by Giambattista Langetti (c. 1660s). It is said of Cato that whenever he is depicted in art it is always in the act of stabbing himself. (Ca' Ressonico, Venice)

- *Jim Smyth is Emeritus Professor of History at the University of Notre Dame.*

FURTHER READING

T. Bartlett, 'The burden of the present: Theobald Wolfe Tone, republican and separatist', in D. Dickson, D. Keogh & K. Whelan (eds), *The United Irishmen: republicanism, radicalism, and rebellion* (Dublin, 1993).

C. Robbins, *The Eighteenth-Century Commonwealthmen* (Cambridge MA, 1959).

J. Smyth, 'Wolfe Tone's Library: the United Irishmen and "Enlightenment"', *Eighteenth-Century Studies* **45** (3) (2012).

TONE THE POLYMATH?
HIS EARLY DUBLIN CLUB LIFE

BY **MARTYN POWELL**

THEOBALD WOLFE TONE is rightly recognised as an immensely talented writer, but though his political pamphlets played a major role in propagating the causes of radicalism, republicanism and Catholic relief (during his lifetime and afterwards), his abilities as a diarist, a memoirist and, within both of these contexts, a comic writer should also be appreciated by historians and literary critics. He was a droll observer of society in Ireland, America and France. In Paris he was disappointed to see a version of *Othello* in which Desdemona was saved at the end: 'I admire a nation that will guillotine sixty people a day for months, men, women and children, and cannot bear the catastrophe of a dramatic exhibition'. One of the most touching elements of his writing focuses on his friendships—particularly with fellow United Irishman Thomas Russell—and upon sociability more generally. Tone was an immensely convivial individual, which perhaps explains some of the frustrations that he found when in exile and good companionship was hard to find.

A COMMITTED CLUBMAN
In his early life Tone was a committed clubman, and a member of the Trinity College Historical Society, the Hibernian Catch Club, the Belfast Washington Club and, of course, the United Irishmen, as well as enjoying the entertainments

Left: Theobald Wolfe Tone in Volunteer uniform—the early years of his associational life, before revolutionary politics became all-encompassing, deserve more attention. (Madden, *United Irishmen*/NLI)

TONE THE POLYMATH? HIS EARLY DUBLIN CLUB LIFE

Above: Thomas Russell—one of the most touching elements of Tone's writing focuses on his friendships, particularly with fellow United Irishman Russell. (Madden, *United Irishmen*/NLI)

Below: Seán O'Faolain—saw Tone as 'the sort of man who must have dreamed as often of the gaiety as of the comfort he could bring to Ireland should his plans succeed'.

offered by the Galway Bucks and the Catholic Committee. Here there were ample opportunities for carousing with friends, for heavy drinking and, less happily, for the dreadful hangovers that followed. These early years of Tone's associational life, before revolutionary politics became all-encompassing, deserve more attention. Comparatively little has been written of Tone's early club-going, and to miss this dimension underplays his importance in Dublin's sociable networks in the early 1790s. Part of his appeal must lie in his undoubted status as, if not a true polymath, someone with very creditable gifts across a number of disciplines—history, political thought, epistolary fiction, comic writing, acting and singing.

Tone must have been terrific company. It is also of critical importance to stress the serious dimensions of sociability—personal relationships forged in spirits of comradery and competition, particularly in the relatively incestuous social spaces of upper-middle-class Dublin, could have life-changing ramifications. Was the fate of another United Irish leader, Henry Sheares, sealed by his romantic trumping of John Fitzgibbon, who later, as lord chancellor, held his life in his hands? In the opposite direction, Tone's ability to go into exile in 1795 was secured in part by his close relationship with the lawyer Marcus Beresford, son of leading parliamentary power broker John Beresford.

To further our understanding of Tone's sociability, and some of his cultural and artistic impulses, we need to look at his formative club and associational life. Early studies of Tone may have veered towards the hagiographic, but they also prefigured the 'emotional turn' in historical writing. Seán O'Faolain saw Tone as 'the sort of man who must have dreamed as often of the gaiety as of the comfort he could bring to Ireland should his plans succeed'. R.R. Madden referred to the 'private intimacy which existed between persons of such incongruous public sentiments, as those members of the first Reform and United Irishmen Societies, the Historical Society, and various clubs and associations of a later date'.

HIBERNIAN CATCH CLUB

We have been left with a particularly good account of some of Tone's

Above: R.R. Madden—referred to the 'private intimacy which existed between persons of such incongruous public sentiments, as those members of the first Reform and United Irishmen Societies, the Historical Society, and various clubs and associations of a later date'.

friendship networks in the early 1790s thanks to his membership of the Hibernian Catch Club—a musical society that is still going strong in Dublin at the time of writing. His diary shows that after a financial windfall he paid for his membership to the club, but we know comparatively little beyond that. Tone's most famous musical comment was his 'strum, strum and be hanged' remark, given in the context of the Belfast harpers' festival in 1792, an episode that has been discussed at some length by historians and literary critics. Some qualifiers are worth referencing here. First, Tone had revealed his knowledge of harp music a couple of days earlier: 'All go to the Harpers at one. Poor enough, ten performers: seven execrable; three good; one of them, Fanning, far the best. No new musical discovery. Believe all the good Irish Airs are already written.' Second, he was most likely hungover on both days of festival attendance, on the second having risen 'again with a head ach[e]'. Third, Tone had native music played at his departure from Ireland. Finally, it is worth adding to the mix that in the context of the Catch Club Tone was happy to be a member of a society that, on occasion, paid for its own harpist. This was a Welshman, 'Evans the Harp', who as well as his own payment secured a bottle of port for the harp. The Hibernian Catch Club employed him in the same year as the Belfast festival, five months afterwards, and so the club was perhaps reacting to this increased interest in traditional Irish music. Tone was not present at the Catch Club on this occasion; he had left a year earlier.

Most revealing about Wolfe Tone's entry to the Catch Club is the rule under which he initially seemed to be considered. This was no ordinary recommendation. Rather it seems that Tone's admission to the club was to be conducted under the auspices of a new rule designed to smooth the passage of particularly gifted singers and avoid the usual rigmarole connected with proposal and potential rejection. Tone clearly had a patron who was convinced of his musical abilities. He would have been expected to perform in front of a select group of the committee's senior singers—several of whom would have been 'professional' vicars choral and members of Dublin's cathedral choirs—and be admitted (or not) as a consequence. Although there is no record of what Tone might have been expected to sing, details of a later test, from 1798, survive—and the candidate was required to support 'to the satisfaction of the committee' a part in nine different glees. Any expenses accrued during the process were to be met by the proposer—an indication that Tone had committed support. In the event the committee required to examine Tone was not set up, and Sir John Ferns (not a catch singer—he was a wine merchant), who had been the club president responsible for putting together the committee, was fined a substantial £1 2s 9d for his failure to do so.

BALLOTED AND ACCEPTED

Tone was initially proposed by Dr James Cleghorn, a medic, and Henry Humphrey, a barrister, under the 'new rule'. Broader acceptability to the club was indicated, however, by the fact that in March 1790 two different members nominated him under the conventional membership route: the printer George Grierson and a military officer, Charles Moore McMahon. Of course, club embarrassment over the administrative cock-up might have played a part here. Nevertheless, on 30 March 1790 Wolfe Tone was balloted for and accepted into the club. Not only did he have backers but also he was without enemies. As for his friends,

TONE THE POLYMATH? HIS EARLY DUBLIN CLUB LIFE

George Grierson was a contemporary of Tone's at Trinity College, and Charles Moore McMahon, a lieutenant from County Carlow, was militarily very well connected (his wife was also from a soldiering family).

It is difficult to gauge the full extent of Tone's attendance, as payment records are only complete for dinner days (occurring once a month), but he did have phases of regular-ish attendance. If a club member failed to turn up and pay his five shillings by eight o'clock on a dinner day he could be excluded, but the president might appeal to other members to cover this, or the half-crown absence fee. Tone was saved on a number of occasions from this ignominy by friends in the club—unlike some of his fellow singers (even some very famous ones, like the composer Sir John Andrew Stephenson).

Tone's involvement with the club in the spring of 1790 coincided with his early pamphleteering and, after taking a house in Irishtown in the summer, his burgeoning friendship with Thomas Russell. The days spent in Irishtown speak to an earlier form of private conviviality, akin to that enjoyed by Jonathan Swift and his circle. Gathered with his wife, Matilda, and Russell were Tone's brother Mathew and Russell's brother John. Tone commented on their witty conversation: 'I know not whether our wit was perfectly classical or not, nor does it signify. If it was not sterling, at least it passed current among ourselves. If I may judge, we were none of us destitute of the humour indigenous in the soil of Ireland.' He continued: 'every day produced a ballad, or some poetical squib, which amused us after dinner'. At the start of the new autumn season, he was again an absentee from the club, but his personal credit remained buoyant and other members were willing to pay his dues—James Cleghorn in October and George Grierson in November.

That Tone was back in the Catch Club's orbit is revealed by the fact that in November he paid the 6½d for his copy of the prize-winning glee. He was then subsidised for an absence by John Whitley Stokes, another barrister, related to Whitley Stokes, a co-founder in Tone's first attempt to form a United Irishmen-type organisation. At the close of the year Cleghorn again paid for him, but this is then crossed out in the account book, indicating that Tone had provided the money himself.

In early 1791 Tone was back at the club, paying the full 4s 4d as his dinner subscription. In the spring he was again absent for the club's dinners, and this time John Farran, an attorney, and Henry Doyel, a barrister, paid for him. The range of backers that he had in the club is impressive—and, like Grierson, Farran and Doyel were influential figures in the association, often being selected to serve on the committees that ran the club's business. Tone did not return to the club—at least for its dinner days—in the autumn of 1791. Cleghorn (three times) and Doyel (once) covered his debts. By the end of the year Tone had resigned, Henry Humphrey paying his final fees. The nature of the surviving dinner lists seems to indicate that when the debts covered were paid, the name of the individual coming forward was crossed out. This did not seem to happen in Tone's case, possibly leaving him somewhat indebted to James Cleghorn in particular.

As we have seen, this grouping—dominated by those in the legal profession—can be traced to Tone via the musical and financial challenges posed by his club membership, but there were also members connected to his politics. David Gelling of Dame Street, a hatter and umbrella manufacturer and a member since 1776, was a United Irishman. Though not overlapping with Tone, Francis Magan, a Catholic lawyer, was another United Irishman, and a government informer during the 1790s.

Above: Leonard McNally—in the 1770s Hibernian Catch Club member Philip Cogan collaborated with the United Irish informer on the comic opera *The Ruling Passion*. (NLI)

In the 1770s Catch Club member Philip Cogan collaborated with another United Irish informer, Leonard McNally, on the comic opera *The Ruling Passion*. John Boardman, a barrister, was friendly with the Sheares brothers and was called as a witness for the defence during their trial; Sir John Ferns was a juror in the same trial, and a friend of United Irish defence lawyer extraordinaire John Philpott Curran. The printer and bookseller Stephen Armitage, whose columns in the radical *Dublin Morning Post* were described as 'very democratic', was a member from 1786 and overlapped with Tone.

NOT ALL RADICALS
This is not to say that the club was dominated by likeminded radicals. Though there were plenty of lawyers, men from Dublin's civic world and others involved in the world of print—all of whom might have known and liked Tone—there was also a distinct group of serious musicians attached to the two cathedrals. The priorities of these groups occasionally clashed, though Tone's seemingly gifted status as a singer may have made him one of the few who bridged the divide. There must also have been political bifurcation, as some members gravitated towards forms of loyalist politics. Four members, among them James Cleghorn, belonged to the Association for Discountenancing Vice, which also included England's arch-radical baiter Hannah Moore.

The United Irishman David Gelling was likely not the best-behaved member of the club. As well as fines for absences while acting as secretary, twice in one month, he was fined 6½d for interrupting a catch in May 1787. In October 1791 there is a reference to a 'wager' won by 'Mr Gelding' of 2s 2d (then crossed out) in the account books. In contrast, Tone seemed to have been reasonably well drilled in catch-club etiquette and avoided the penalties meted out for a range of infractions—many administrative, but others concerned with politeness. As Gelling found to his cost, fines were levied for interrupting a musical performance, and leading members were not excused. Tone's friend George Grierson was fined for speaking in October 1786. Charles Martin was fined for speaking in November 1786, and then for interrupting a catch in November 1787. Robert Small, who was supposed to have been part of the musical panel due to test Tone, was fined for interrupting a catch in November 1790. There were also fines for late arrivals, as was the case for Anthony Thompson, coming late twice in December 1786.

'A SOBER MAN'?
Tone's resignation from the Catch Club at the end of 1791 certainly makes sense when other factors are considered. In August 1791 he published his *Argument on behalf of the Catholics of Ireland*, 'by a Northern Whig'. It was a huge success, selling thousands of copies in Dublin, Belfast and beyond. His trip to Belfast in the autumn resulted in the formation of the Society of United Irishmen, along with Thomas Russell, Samuel Neilson and others. He then returned to Dublin and, in the company of James

---

'Drink like a fish till past 12 … go to bed as drunk as a Lord. It is downright scandalous to see in this and other journals how often that occurrence takes place—yet I call myself a sober man!'

Napper Tandy and Simon Butler, formed the Dublin version of the society. Inveterate clubman and sociable being that he was, it is difficult to imagine Tone finding the time for his attendance-spotting, fine-happy musical club-mates. Indeed, late 1791 saw Tone's diaries offer one of the great comic voices on the experience of drunkenness. We have his recollections of hangovers, accounts of double vision, attempts—with a nudge and a wink—to blame illness on the food he had eaten, and promises to himself and his amused reader never to do it again (until the next time Russell called!). Typical entries in his diary would see Tone 'rise with a great headach [*sic*]' (this was his first time with the harpers), 'rise as sick as a Dog' and, most alarmingly, 'waken drunk'. On another occasion he recorded, with a good deal of self-awareness: 'Drink like a fish till past 12 … go to bed as drunk as a Lord. It is downright scandalous to see in this and other journals how often that occurrence takes place—yet I call myself a sober man!' At a dinner with United Irish leaders, Tone found 'on looking at Hamilton Rowan that he has got four eyes', and that though himself was 'fixed, but everything about him moving in a rapid rotation'. Moreover, when he 'essays to cross the room', he 'finds it impossible to move rectilineally'. Tone showed a very modern perception of his drunkenness and the potential excuses that could be offered, such as that he was 'perfectly sober, but perceives that everyone else is getting very drunk', and that his inebriated state proceeded 'entirely from having taken a sprig of watercress with his bread at dinner'. The next day he was 'Sick as Demogorgon. Purpose to leave off watercresses with my bread.'

And yet it is important to recognise that sociability alone was insufficient for Tone. The Catch Club contained many big drinkers. Sir John Ferns, (dis)organiser of Tone's failed examination, was said 'to have drunk as much port and claret in his day as would float a seventy-four', a reference to the 74-gun ship of the line popular in the second half of the eighteenth century. Two of Ireland's most brilliant musical stars of the eighteenth century and Catch Club members—John Andrew Stephenson (who collaborated with Thomas Moore) and John Spray—

TONE THE POLYMATH? HIS EARLY DUBLIN CLUB LIFE

Above: Composer Sir John Andrew Stephenson was once fined by the Hibernian Catch Club for failure to attend one of its dinners. (NPG, London)

enjoyed bibulous sessions that became legendary. Or, more specifically, on 7 March 1809 we find that there were only two members present but they still managed to drink six bottles of claret between them—costing £2 5s 6d. One of the great bugbears of its musical leaders was to find that, after paying a sizeable bill for an evening of gourmandising, a number of members had stayed on and ordered several more bottles of claret or port and not paid. During Tone's time a 'whip' that would have dealt with such practices was banned by the club.

Tone needed more, however, than frivolity (even with musical accompaniment). When he formed 'a kind of political club' with Drennan and Thomas Addis Emmett in late 1790, he confessed that 'our meetings degenerated into downright, ordinary suppers. We became a mere oyster club.' For Tone, conviviality had to have political bite. When he met Thomas Russell and Samuel Neilson in an alehouse in November 1791 they combined drinking with a discussion of Joseph Priestley's response to Tone's *Argument on behalf of the Catholics*. On other occasions it is difficult not to be carried away by Tone's political enthusiasm when in his cups. After dinner at Belfast's Donegall Arms we are given: 'Huzza! God bless everybody! Stanislaus Augustus! Geo. Washington! Beau jour! Who would have thought it this morning? Huzza! Generally drunk. Broke my glass thumping the table. Home, god knows how, or when. Huzza! God bless every one again, generally.'

Did Tone leave the Catch Club because of failures in its sociable diversions (or possibly even its musical ones)? On 23 February 1790 only two members attended the ordinary weekly meeting, and on 2 March there were only four members. He may have wondered whether his money was well spent (if indeed he had turned up himself). Life with Thomas Russell must have seemed far more fulfilling. Amusingly, Tone's friend George Grierson ended up as the only member dining at one Catch Club dinner in November 1812. Grierson dutifully filled in the account book: 'The President having read to *himself* the Proceedings of the last Dinner Day resolved to eat one quarter of a hundred of excellent and curious Carlingford oysters, to drink a pint of porter and a tumbler of pottieen punch; which was accordingly done to the great satisfaction of the *present* company'. After 10 o'clock, '(no other business having occurred), the President adjourned the meeting till the following Tuesday evening—after drinking his own health with three times three'. Grierson's experience reveals the limitations of Dublin's club-based conviviality for men like Tone, and why the United Irish movement gave both sociable as well as political succour. The reference to poteen, though, reminds us of the way in which older Irish modes were taken up by bodies that were predominantly Protestant. Tone would not have begrudged the harp its bottle of port.

- *Martyn J. Powell is Head of the School of Humanities at the University of Bristol.*

FURTHER READING

N. Curtin, *The United Irishmen: popular politics in Ulster and Dublin, 1791–1798* (Oxford, 1998).

M. Elliott, *Wolfe Tone: prophet of Irish independence* (2nd edn) (Liverpool, 2012).

J. Kelly & M.J. Powell (eds), *Clubs and societies in eighteenth-century Ireland* (Dublin, 2010).

R.R. Madden, *The United Irishmen, their lives and times* (7 vols) (1842–60).

T. O'Hanlon, 'The Hibernian Catch Club: catch and glee culture in Georgian and Victorian Dublin', *Journal of the Society for Musicology in Ireland* **13** (2018), 17–33.

'THE TEST OF EVERY MAN'S POLITICAL CREED'—

BY **ULTÁN GILLEN**

WOLFE TONE AND THE FRENCH REVOLUTION

IN PARIS IN AUGUST 1796, a *chef de brigade* (colonel) in the army of the revolutionary French Republic sat down to write his autobiography, expecting that he would soon be accompanying one of France's best and most famous generals, Lazare Hoche, on an invasion fleet destined for Ireland. Theobald Wolfe Tone set out to explain how he had come to hold his commission, and how Ireland had become ripe for the revolution he hoped the invasion would foment. Recalling 1790, he wrote:

Below: Thomas Paine—in his autobiography, Tone claimed that the controversy stirred up by Paine's *Rights of man*, in response to Edmund Burke's *Reflections on the revolution in France*, 'changed in an instant the politics of Ireland.'

'The French Revolution had now been above a twelvemonth in its progress. At its commencement, as the first emotions are generally honest, everyone was in its favour; but after some time the probable consequences to monarchy and aristocracy began to be foreseen, and the partisans of both to retrench considerably in their admiration. At length Mr Burke's famous invective appeared, and this in due season produced Payne's reply, which he called *The rights of man* [sic]. This controversy, and the gigantic event which gave rise to it, changed in an instant the politics of Ireland.'

'In a little time', Tone wrote, 'the French revolution became the test of every man's political creed, and the nation was fairly divided into two great parties, the Aristocrats and the Democrats (epithets borrowed from France).'

For Tone, then, the course of events due to culminate in Hoche's planned invasion began with a debate over what lessons the French Revolution held for other countries, and would end, he hoped, with the creation of an Irish sister republic for revolutionary France, liberating not just the Irish people but also the world from the baleful influence of the British Empire, and securing democracy's victory over aristocracy. What, then, was the French Revolution's impact on Tone at a personal and political level, and what can it tell us about his politics, his character and the relationship between the two?

'THE TEST OF EVERY MAN'S POLITICAL CREED'—WOLFE TONE AND THE FRENCH REVOLUTION

'OUR SUCCESS DEPENDS ON THEIRS'

While the Burke–Paine debate undoubtedly had a major impact on Irish politics, that impact reflected the fact that the French Revolution had already become a major focus of Irish political debate and already fascinated Irish public opinion. A quick glance at an Irish newspaper from the period shows this—indeed, claiming privileged access to information from France soon became an advertising tactic aimed at driving up subscriptions and general sales. Content related to the French Revolution made up a good deal of the average newspaper edition's reporting, especially in the provinces, where distinguishing one's paper from the Dublin journals could be achieved by a smaller focus on the Irish parliament and greater coverage of international affairs. This content ranged from extensive reports of the debates in the French National Assembly to eyewitness accounts and letters from residents of, or visitors to, France, and attempts to interpret the Revolution's lessons for Ireland.

Tone was right that the fall of the Bastille was initially welcomed across the political spectrum, but it took less than a month after that news reached Ireland for the first hostile comments on French events to appear in the conservative press. A particular bugbear for Irish conservatives was any suggestion that the French Revolution provided positive examples that should be emulated. While their liberal and radical opponents repeatedly cited France as a model to follow, conservatives quickly identified its principles as subversive of hierarchy and order. Debates in the press were also echoed in coffee-houses and elsewhere.

> **'A particular bugbear for Irish conservatives was any suggestion that the French Revolution provided positive examples that should be emulated.'**

The core arguments of Burke (that the French Revolution threatened the social and political order) and Paine (that its principles and practices offered a model for achieving genuine freedom) were evident in Irish politics before either put pen to paper. We must also remember that the French Revolution was not an event but a process. The storming of the Bastille produced a constitutional monarchy, not a republic. That came only with the overthrow of the monarchy on 10 August 1792 (called by some historians the Second Revolution) and the subsequent declaration of the Republic in September. Revolutionary France had declared war on Prussia and the Habsburg Empire in April 1792, and the radicalisation that followed until the execution of Robespierre in July 1794 owed much to the consequences of the war. Irish newspapers followed the various twists and turns of the Revolution in great detail.

Such coverage allowed Irish people to feel involved in the French Revolution. The great Belfast Bastille Day celebrations of 1791 and 1792 (during the period of the constitutional monarchy) exemplify this sense of participation. Irish feelings about France were intensified by the Burke–Paine debate and helped drive the polarisation of Irish politics during the early 1790s, though of course domestic events such as the Catholic Convention and militia riots were fundamental to that process. For Tone, the fate of the United Irishmen was bound up with that of France even before the French declared war on Britain in February 1793. In 1792, the year he helped revive the Volunteers as a republican 'National Battalion' that sought to arm radical Catholics as well as Protestants and Dissenters and the poor, he declared that 'everything depends on the line they may take. Our success depends on theirs, which some of us are such fools as not to see.'

Long before he became involved with the French agent Revd William Jackson or resolved to travel to France to seek an alliance, Tone was convinced that the United Irishmen's prospects depended on the French Revolution. It is no surprise, therefore, that he used France to reinforce the message of his most famous and influential work, *An argument on behalf of the Catholics of Ireland*.

The VOLUNTEERS of the CITY and COUNTY of DUBLIN, as they met on COLLEGE GREEN: the 4th of Nov 1779

Above: 'The Volunteers of the City and County of Dublin as they met on College Green: the 4th of Nov 1779'—Tone was raised in a political culture heavily influenced by classical republicanism and that idealised the citizen-soldiers of the Irish Volunteers of 1778–82. In 1792 he sought to revive the Volunteers as a republican National Battalion. (Alamy)

FRANCE AND *AN ARGUMENT ON BEHALF OF THE CATHOLICS OF IRELAND*

The genesis of the *Argument* lies in Belfast's Bastille Day celebrations of 1791. At the invitation of his closest friend, Thomas Russell, and his radical allies in Belfast, Tone wrote resolutions for a new political club intended to emerge from the celebration. The resolutions argued, first, that English influence was a great grievance; second, that the most effectual way to oppose it was to give the people greater political weight through parliamentary reform; third, that no reform could be just or efficacious unless it included the Catholics, although this was, he noted, only insinuated.

Tone thought that the resolutions 'conceded very far indeed to what I consider as vulgar and ignorant prejudices', but even his intimations about the Catholics proved too radical. The resolutions were rejected

HISTORY IRELAND/ 25

'THE TEST OF EVERY MAN'S POLITICAL CREED'—WOLFE TONE AND THE FRENCH REVOLUTION

and the club never appeared. Enraged, Tone wrote the *Argument* in response. When it came to the right of the people to reform the constitution, the *Argument* stated, 'after Paine, who will, or will need to be, heard on the subject?' It was common for supporters of the status quo to argue that Catholics could not be trusted with political power—that the principles of their religion meant that they would use it to oppress Protestants and institute tyranny. Against this, Tone pointed not just to Paine on the principles of the French Revolution but also to its practice.

France, he argued, was a Catholic nation, but the Revolution demonstrated that it understood the theory and practice of the rights of man better than any other. For example, the French National Assembly had instituted religious equality. This was a calculated, though still implicit, attack on the hegemonic belief in official political culture in Ireland and Britain that the British constitution made for perfect freedom. He was arguing that the confessional nature of the Irish state brought not freedom but oppression for the vast majority of its people. The French Revolution brought liberty for all, the Williamite Revolution oppression for the majority.

For Tone, the French Revolution's treatment of the Catholic Church, which had been deprived of its political power and subjected to reforms by the National Assembly on revolutionary principles, demonstrated that scare stories about Catholic tyranny over Protestants could be discounted. The pope had been burnt in effigy in Paris for his opposition to the Revolution, and neither French nor Irish 'emancipated and liberal' Catholics would listen to 'the rusty and extinguished thunderbolts of the Vatican'. Irish Protestant fears of Catholics were therefore proven groundless.

Not content with attacking 1688, the foundation of British and Irish official political culture, he also derided the 'Revolution of 1782', which had achieved (apparent) legislative independence, as 'the most bungling, imperfect business that ever threw ridicule on a lofty epithet'. Though the comparison was not explicitly made, the *Argument* clearly took the view that what France had was a real revolution, which was what Ireland needed, even if Tone presented it as achievable simply and peacefully.

In response to the idea that the Catholics deserved to be free but were not yet ready, an argument often found among Whigs such as those who had rejected his Belfast resolutions, Tone said that had the French waited for the entire population to be ready for liberty they would still be slaves. For him, revolutionary France was the trump card that demonstrated the failings of the existing system and the limitations of moderate reformers.

The *Argument*'s final paragraph states that the 'example of America, of Poland and above all of France, cannot, on the minds of liberal men, but force conviction'. All Irish reformers needed to do was 'once cry *Reform and the Catholics*, and Ireland is free, independent and happy'. In other words, other revolutions, most of all France's, had shown how to put political power in the hands of the people: mobilise public opinion, put aside internal divisions and use the power that numbers gave. With that done, success lay within their grasp.

The *Argument* proved immensely influential. There is no doubt that it convinced many Protestant radicals in Ulster that Catholics could be trusted with political power, and it seems highly likely that Tone's use of the French Revolution helped make that case. The *Argument* also showed how Tone's own politics had broken the bounds of the political culture in which he was raised. While the Whigs spoke of perfecting the constitution, Tone, already a separatist, had reached the conclusion that a different type of constitution organised on different principles—the rights of man—was necessary, even if public opinion was such that that could only be hinted at rather than stated as baldly as he would have liked. For him, 1789 outshone the foundational events of official Irish political culture, revealing their fundamental flaws and limitations.

MASCULINITY AND REVOLUTION

Tone's political life can only be understood by grasping the centrality of his vision of masculinity to his behaviour. In political terms, as someone raised in a political culture heavily influenced by classical republicanism and that idealised the citizen-soldiers of the Irish Volunteers of 1778–82, this meant stepping forward to do what he considered his duty. While he certainly had other motivations for his political activity, not least ambition, his sense of what he considered his manly duty and masculine self lay at the heart of his political choices. This helps explain his decision to join the United Irishmen and play a prominent role in their activities, despite the risks to his career, and why, when James Napper Tandy's dispute with Solicitor General John Toler threatened to expose the United Irishmen to government repression and to risk the impugnment of their honour (Tandy being widely regarded as having ducked a duel), he stepped forward to save their honour and demonstrate that they would not be intimidated.

As the United Irishmen continued to spread their French-inspired political message, Tone's masculinity at other points shaped his political

> 'France, he argued, was a Catholic nation, but the Revolution demonstrated that it understood the theory and practice of the rights of man better than any other.'

actions. In late 1792 the United Irishmen sought to revive the Volunteers as an additional means of mobilising public opinion and, in Ulster at least, there is evidence that revolutionaries like Samuel Neilson hoped to transform them into the nucleus of any future armed revolution.

The right to bear arms was connected to citizenship in Irish political culture, with Catholics still formally banned from owning arms in 1792. Tone, by winter 1792 effectively the agent of the Catholic Committee, was busy organising the Catholic Convention. The system for electing its members of 'one man, one vote' and indirect election looked a lot like that of the French Republic, something its enemies were quick to point out. Tone's democratic impulses also found expression in his role in creating the National Battalion.

The National Battalion, founded in November 1792, had a uniform deliberately modelled on that of the French Revolution's citizen militia, the National Guards. The uniform was designed to be affordable to the lower classes. Catholics were also welcome to join. Moreover, its insignia, designed by Tone, were republican, with the harp not only without the crown but also underneath the cap of liberty, the *bonnet rouge* beloved of the Parisian *sans-culottes*. The message was unmistakable. This was an armed body formed according to the principles of revolutionary democracy embodied by the new French Republic. It is little wonder that the government soon moved to ban the Volunteers.

The Battalion failed to get off the ground, which Tone attributed to others involved lacking his enthusiasm for it, but we see how his masculine sense of duty merged seamlessly with his revolutionary politics. In the case of Volunteering, it also merged with a desire that he had harboured since boyhood of being a soldier. The French Republic finally made his dream come true in 1796.

TONE IN PARIS
After arriving in France in February 1796, a lonely Tone rapidly developed the habit of attending the theatre, which provided not just entertainment but also solace and political inspiration. The night after reaching Paris, it transported him into a state of emotional and political ecstasy as his ideal self-image and political principles came alive on stage. A performance celebrating liberty and the republic moved him deeply. The crowd singing the Marseillaise 'affected me most powerfully', while this man of eighteenth-century sensibility found the sight of children kneeling at an altar of liberty and kindling torches from its fire 'at once pathetic and sublime beyond what I had ever seen'. Yet it was what followed that rendered the scene 'a spectacle worthy of a free republic'. As the words '*Aux armes, Citoyens*' rang out, National Guardsmen, bayonets fixed, sabres drawn, *tricolore* flying, rushed on stage:

'It would be impossible to describe the effect of this. I never knew what enthusiasm was before, and what heightened it beyond all conception was that the men I saw before me were not hirelings acting a part; they were what they seemed, French citizens flying to arms to rescue their country from slavery; they were the men who had precipitated Coburg into the Sambre and driven Clairfait over

Above: The foyer of the Montansier Theatre in Paris, *c.* 1798. After arriving in France in February 1796, Tone regularly attended the theatre. (Bibliothèque nationale de France)

the Rhine, and were now on the eve of again hurrying to the frontiers to encounter fresh dangers and gain fresh glory. *This* was what made the spectacle interesting beyond all description. I would willingly sail again from New York to enjoy again what I felt at that moment.'

Tone's political principles, the heroes who had repeatedly defeated the agents of tyranny, the symbols of revolutionary masculinity, were on stage before him—the sight moved him beyond anything else. It reaffirmed his faith in the Revolution, his mission, his politics and himself. It tied him emotionally to the French people in a way that he had not been before.

That September, he both fulfilled a lifelong dream and joined his heroes when he was commissioned as an officer of the army of the French Republic. Putting on his uniform made him 'as pleased as a little boy in his first breeches: foolish enough, but not unpleasant. Walked about Paris to shew myself. Huzza! Citizen Wolfe Tone, chef de brigade in the service of the Republic!'

The uniform of the French army,

'THE TEST OF EVERY MAN'S POLITICAL CREED'—WOLFE TONE AND THE FRENCH REVOLUTION

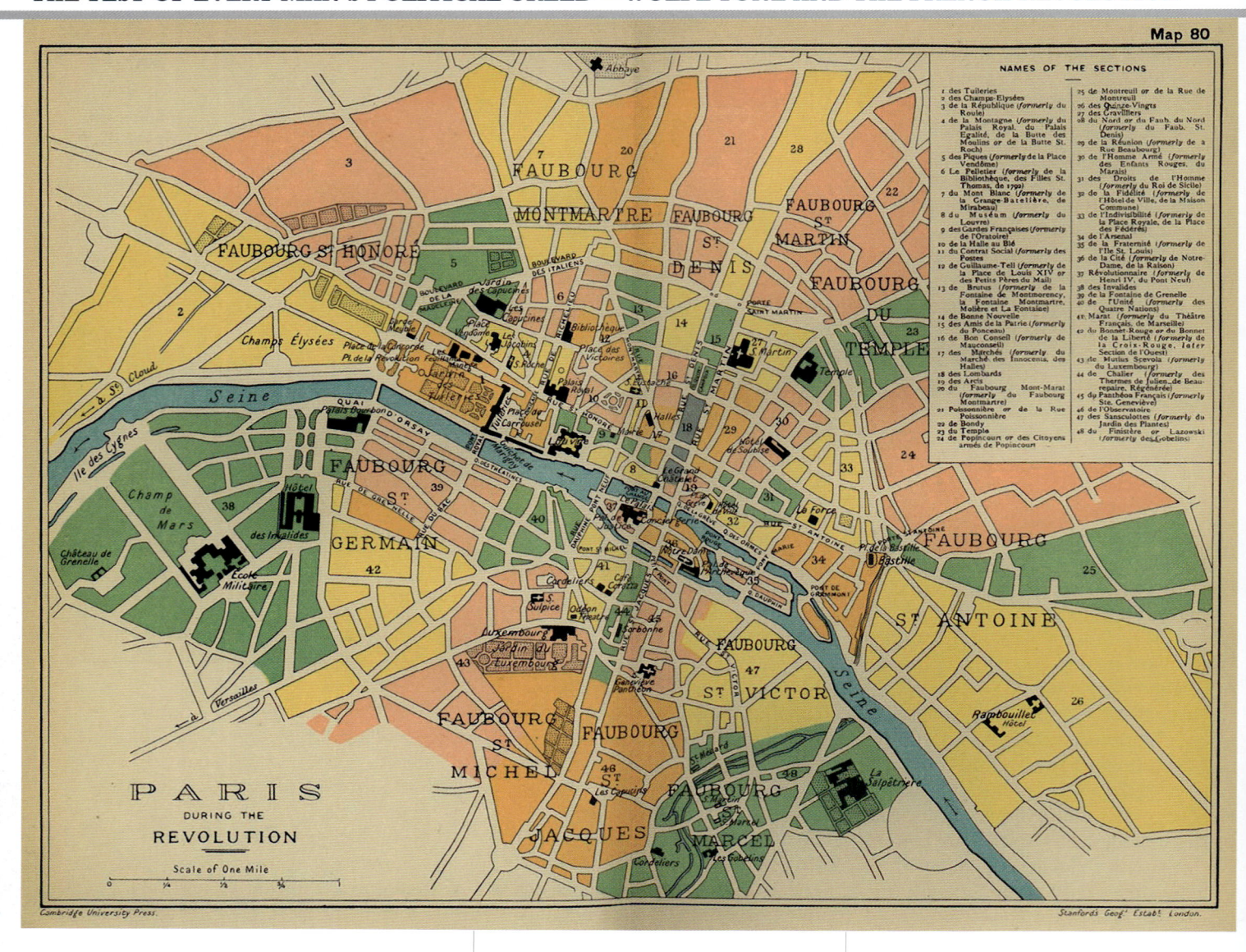

the acceptance he found from Hoche and the other officers, and the feelings of masculine pride and satisfaction they brought help explain Tone's decision to face his trial in 1798 dressed in his finest French uniform (though this was also part of a legal strategy, which he knew was likely to fail, to try to avoid execution by claiming French citizenship). There seems little doubt that he felt at his most complete as a man and a revolutionary when wearing his uniform.

CONCLUSION

Tone's connection to the French Revolution operated at many different levels—ideological, pragmatic and emotional. Its ideas inspired him, seeming to offer the means of breaking the sectarian log-jam of Irish history; its power offered the means to break the connection with England; and the emotional fulfilment of serving the cause of revolution in Ireland and France brought immense satisfaction, despite the lonely and difficult times. The French Revolution brought together Tone's sense of the type of man he wanted to be, of the politics he held and of the future he wanted to build. That imagined future was not just about Ireland but about a whole new civilisation for Europe and further afield, where French and Irish revolutionary democrats, and their allies elsewhere, would build a new and better world.

Tone failed and accepted his failure. As he told the court, he had done his duty and would accept the consequences. His connection to and involvement with the French Revolution meant that he died feeling not just that he had passed the test of every man's political creed but also that he had passed the test of what it meant to be a man.

• *Ultán Gillen lectures in History at Teesside University.*

FURTHER READING

M. Elliott, *Partners in revolution: the United Irishmen and France* (Yale, 1982).

A. Forrest & M. Middell (eds), *The Routledge companion to the French Revolution in world history* (Abingdon, 2016).

U. Gillen, 'Democracy, religion, and the political thought of Theobald Wolfe Tone', *History of European Ideas* 46 (7) (2020).

S. Maslan, *Revolutionary acts: theatre, democracy, and the French Revolution* (Chicago, 2005).

WOLFE TONE'S BELFAST RELATIONSHIPS AND THEIR INFLUENCES

BY **KENNETH L. DAWSON**

Above: The Volunteers of Belfast celebrate Bastille Day on 14 July 1792. Tone observed that 'The Dissenters of the north, and especially from the town of Belfast, are, from the genius of their religion, and from the superior diffusion of political information among them, sincere and enlightened republicans'. (NLI)

WRITING IN HIS PARIS memoir of 1796, Theobald Wolfe Tone declared nostalgically that the three weeks he spent in Belfast in October 1791 were ones that he looked back on 'as perhaps the most pleasantest in my life'. His visit was a purposeful one, an opportunity to meet those advanced political radicals known to him only by renown. Similarly, these northern Dissenters were keen to invite Tone to their town, his reputation as a political commentator and agitator having been cemented by the publication of his *Argument on behalf of the Catholics of Ireland* just two months before. With a new reform society due to be launched in Belfast, Tone's visit to meet his new Presbyterian followers was facilitated by his friend Thomas Russell, who had been stationed there the previous year as an ensign with the 64th Regiment of Foot. Tone's arrival was not, therefore, so much a historical blind date as a meeting of minds. He found the town very much to his liking: small and compact, industrious, self-confident and convivial. His journal, a fine example of this relatively novel medium, recalled—albeit hazily—late nights and excessive drinking, but also serious political discussion and important details about the formation of the Society of United Irishmen, a seminal moment in Irish history. Whilst Tone's impact on Belfast was self-evident, he would in turn be influenced by the place he termed 'Blefescu', not just by his stays there in 1791, 1792 and 1795 but also by what he learned about the place before his first visit.

BIRTHPLACE OF THE VOLUNTEERS

Tone arrived in a town of around 18,320 people, the birthplace of the Volunteers back in 1778, whose more progressive citizens increasingly sympathised with the extension of greater political rights to Catholics. This was a town where familial and denominational ties with those in the vanguard of the American Revolution meant that terms such as representation, citizenship and natural rights became part of the political lexicon. An overwhelmingly Presbyterian town, two of the three meeting-houses in Rosemary Lane did not subscribe to the Westminster Confession of Faith, the first congregation having been served in the past by the Revd Thomas Drennan, whose son, William, conceived the idea of a reform society that embraced genuine and inclusive reform, with the greatest happiness of the greatest number at its core. In 1791, members of this congregation included men such as William Tennent and Thomas McCabe, who would become leading members of the Society of United Irishmen. But it was not just the 'New Light' that embraced political innovation in Belfast. Revd Sinclare Kelburn ministered the third, trinitarian, congregation, whose members included the Brysons, Biggers, Neilsons, Simms and McCrackens—all prominent names in the United Irishmen.

Presbyterians rejected ecclesiastical hierarchy and promoted individual relationships with God through a close reading of scripture. The town's literacy levels were higher than many other urban centres, with a Reading Society that evolved into the Belfast Society for Promoting Knowledge and a philanthropic spirit that promoted the principle of urban improvement.

With Belfast's two MPs being the appointees of the Marquess of Donegall, as well as the town sovereign and a select few burgesses, the excluded Presbyterian mercantile class may have been assigned their place, but they refused to accept it. Inspired by events unfolding in Paris in 1789, the most progressive Belfast

> *'Attacks on a monopolistic French ruling class and a privileged State church resonated with many of the politically disenfranchised ... '*

citizens rallied to the banner of serious reform. Attacks on a monopolistic French ruling class and a privileged State church resonated with many of the politically disenfranchised, and Thomas Paine's *Rights of man*—which Tone deemed the 'Koran of Belfast'—was purchased individually or read collectively. With interest in reform politics revived, the Volunteers of Belfast were once again on the march.

It was into this environment that Tone would be welcomed enthusiastically by many of the town's citizens in 1791. He observed in his journal that his fellow travellers were 'all steady, sensible, clear men, and as I judge, extremely well adapted for serious business'. He would later write that 'The Dissenters of the north, and especially from the town of Belfast, are, from the genius of their religion, and from the superior diffusion of political information among them, sincere and enlightened republicans'.

SUSPICION OF CATHOLICS

Tone also observed, however, that these Belfast radicals were largely ignorant of Catholics and of the now more dynamic Catholic Committee. Traditional doctrinal suspicions of Catholicism prevailed, and Tone would later note that he had work to do to convert even the radical Dissenters to his arguments, centred on the need for a fundamental reform of parliament that included Irishmen of every religious persuasion. Tone was certainly shaped by Belfast influences, but he also helped to redefine Belfast, challenging old prejudices and acting as a persuader for a form of politics which, while not altogether new in embracing parliamentary reform and demanding the removal of sectarian divisions, was innovative in highlighting that Catholics were, in fact, capable of political liberty and not slaves to what was viewed (not least by Tone himself) as superstition and priestcraft. The lessons of the French Revolution had unlocked the sectarian stalemate that had thwarted earlier calls for reform in Ireland. It was at this point that Tone's relationships cultivated within the town of Belfast provided him with the influence he needed to effectuate his plans.

THOMAS RUSSELL

Two of the most significant influences on Tone's developing philosophy were men who were only temporarily resident in Belfast—Thomas Russell and the American Thomas Attwood Digges. After their meeting in the gallery of the Irish parliament in 1790, Tone and Russell became firm friends. The former's journal, memoir and letters contain numerous references to their incredibly close friendship and the unique political synergy created by their discussions. The idyllic summer that Tone, his wife Matilda and Russell enjoyed in Irishtown in 1790 ended when the latter was posted to Belfast. Tone, himself the aspiring soldier, seemed at that time more interested in Russell's uniform than in his destination, but Russell's deployment was educational for him, and Tone became familiar with the town's political and religious

Above: Thomas Attwood Digges—in Belfast he offered Tone an American perspective on Ireland's politics, and a lived experience of declaring independence from London and taking up arms against the king.

dynamics through their communications. When in July 1791 Tone drafted resolutions for the events in Belfast commemorating the second anniversary of the storming of the Bastille, the third, relating to reform that would include the Catholics, touched a nerve and was fudged. It was at this stage that Tone wrote about becoming a 'red-hot Catholic' and he began to address the concerns of those descendants of Scottish and English settlers who traditionally viewed Catholics with suspicion.

Tone's audience for his famous 1791 *Argument* were the northern Dissenters. He was informed and influenced by Russell's intimate knowledge of Belfast. In his own scribbled journal, months earlier, Russell challenged the common objections against Catholic relief: the sheer number of beneficiaries of reform; their perceived attachment to a foreign ecclesiastical power; fears of a property transformation if Catholics were empowered; and the likelihood of future religious conflict and its consequences. While Tone's *Argument* showcased his very considerable gift for pamphleteering, he was relying on Russell's identification of a northern myopia as far as Catholics were concerned. The two men were together in Dublin in the summer of 1791, during which Russell's influence on Tone's philosophy was likely at its zenith. Tone was now forewarned and intellectually forearmed, enabling him to woo Presbyterian sceptics by celebrating the Revolution's attack on the Catholic Church in France. This allowed Presbyterian radicals to speculate about the potential asset of securing lapsed Catholics to their campaign (the extent of Catholic devotion arguably existing more in their minds than in those of Catholics themselves). Becoming a lapsed Presbyterian was not, however, countenanced, since many of them viewed the French Revolution as a vindication of scriptural prophecy rather than a call to deism.

THOMAS ATTWOOD DIGGES

Another influence on Tone during his first sojourn in Belfast was Thomas Attwood Digges. A neighbour and friend of George Washington, who lived on the other side of the Potomac River, Digges was variously a political go-between, an industrial pirate and someone who aroused the suspicions of none other than Benjamin Franklin, who regarded him as a scoundrel at best. No stranger to a prison cell, Digges features regularly in Tone's 1791 journal. Out walking, at breakfast and dinner with Digges during his three-week stay in Belfast, Tone's thinking was undoubtedly shaped, for Digges offered an American perspective on Ireland's politics, as well as a lived experience of declaring independence from London and taking up arms against the king. Digges helped Tone to crystallise his thinking on a political pathway, namely that Ireland had the capacity for independence and—crucially—that for any chance of success in this endeavour England needed to be distracted by war, with the concomitant possibility that France would be sympathetic to any attempt to subvert English influence in Ireland, or anywhere else for that matter. Digges's thoughts, approved of at this time by the United Irish-man and entrepreneur William Sinclaire, were that 'If Ireland were free and well governed being that she is unencumbered with debt, she would, in arts, commerce and manufacturing spring up like an air balloon and leave England behind her at an immense difference. There is no computing the rapidity with which she would rise.' This Swiftian analysis of Ireland's economic potential was not new, but in 1791 it tapped into Tone's existing thinking, addressed briefly in his earlier pamphlet, *Spanish war!* (1790). When Tone discovered that Digges had been arres-ted in Glasgow in 1792 after stealing pieces of muslin on a shopping excursion, he declared in his diary: 'Digges, the *hero* [my italics] of my last journal, a shoplifter!' Digges's influence on Tone predicted the trajectory of the United Irishmen and added an international

WOLFE TONE'S BELFAST RELATIONSHIPS AND THEIR INFLUENCES

Above: Samuel Neilson, labelled 'The Jacobin' in Tone's Belfast journal, was a major influence. (National Museums NI)

perspective that other figures were less likely to have.

SAMUEL NEILSON

Tone was influenced, educated and frequently annoyed by other key figures in Belfast from 1791 right through to his departure from Ireland in June 1795. His journals and letters highlight figures such as Thomas McCabe, William Sinclaire and Robert and William Simms, the latter respected for their financial generosity as well as their political activism. Unsurprisingly, Samuel Neilson, the Belfast cotton merchant, was a major influence on Tone. A member of the First Belfast Volunteer Company—the 'Green Company'—Neilson's commanding officer was Captain Waddell Cunningham, known to be opposed to immediate Catholic relief. Neilson's role as one of the leading organisers and strategists of the United Irishmen is well documented.

Above: Waddell Cunningham—'a lying old scoundrel' according to Tone—was opposed to immediate Catholic relief. (National Museums NI)

In what cannot be regarded as a coincidence, he was in Dublin and met with William Drennan on 20 May 1791, the day before Drennan wrote the famous letter to his brother-in-law in Belfast, Samuel McTier, about the potential formation of a new political society, and it was Neilson who took the lead in establishing the *Northern Star* newspaper, plans for which were well under way before Tone's arrival in Belfast in October. Moreover, the fact that Tone labelled Neilson 'The Jacobin' in his journal, when most others were given names associated with their professions, speaks volumes about both his radicalism and his influence. It was Neilson who reminded Tone that Belfast had a strong reformist tradition and how many of its citizens had been receptive to parliamentary reform and the extension of political rights to Catholics in the previous decade. Although the town's radicalism was demonstrable, Tone had only recently come to see the potential of the northern Dissenters.

Before the first full meeting of the new society, Tone dined at Neilson's house and the two men set off together. No record of their conversation exists but it is likely to have included Neilson telling Tone his plans for how the meeting should unfold, in the same way as he tried to influence the direction of the Catholic Convention from Belfast in December 1792. When he did not get his own way on the latter occasion, the surly Neilson fired verbal salvos towards Tone and the leading Catholic, Richard McCormick. Neilson was also at the centre of Tone's farewells in Belfast in the summer of 1795—climbing the Cave Hill and pledging at its summit 'never to desist in our efforts until we had subverted the authority of England over our country', picnicking in the deer-park and camping on Ram's Island in Lough Neagh. When Tone departed for America and thence to France, Neilson and the Belfast set acted quickly to fulfil their side of the bargain. If we are to believe the deposition offered by William Hart of Carrickfergus in September 1795, Neilson had attempted communication with the French National Assembly, Russell had been given the command of the emerging United Irish military structure in Ulster, arms were being procured and 10,000 men had been recruited across Antrim and Down. Tone left Ireland in no doubt about the determination of the Belfast leadership—this self-styled Committee of General Welfare—and its accelerating strategy.

UNWITTING INFLUENCERS

As well as being influenced by advocates of radical reform in Belfast, Tone's politics were shaped by those

Below: McArt's Fort, Cave Hill, overlooking Belfast, where in June 1795 Tone, Russell, Neilson, Henry Joy McCracken and Robert Simms swore an oath 'never to desist in our efforts until we had subverted the authority of England over our country'. (Alamy)

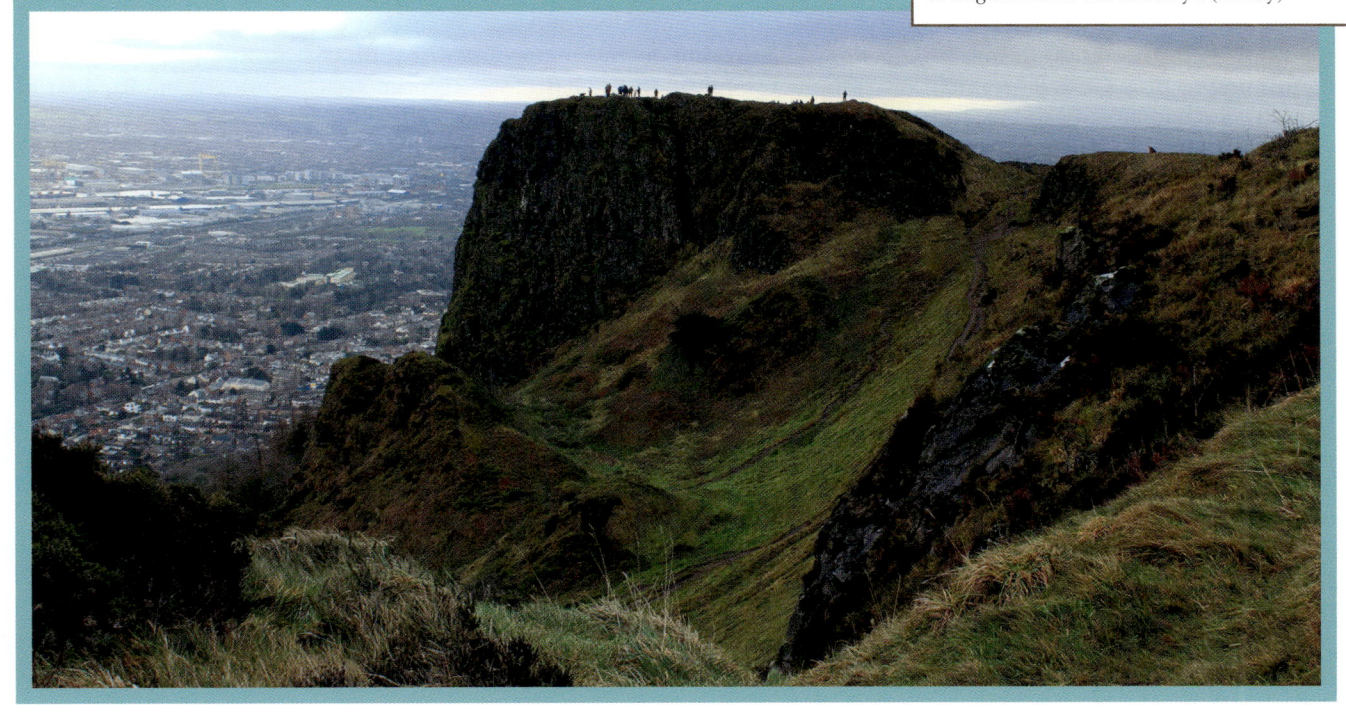

HISTORY IRELAND/ **33**

who were opposed to increasing political rights for Catholics and whose hardened positions on the subject he hoped to dismantle. Not all Belfast Presbyterians were as advanced in their thinking as those who became members of the United Irishmen, a fact which helps to explain why Neilson and others found it necessary to operate a secret Volunteer committee during 1791 to conduct their affairs. The more cautious Presbyterians were reflective of the membership of the Northern Whig Club, with the minister of the 'First' congregation, Revd William Bruce, the physician Dr Alexander Halliday, the editor of the whiggish *Belfast News-Letter* Henry Joy junior and the leading Volunteer, Waddell Cunningham, refusing to get carried away by notions of Catholic enfranchisement and emancipation. These men were not altogether reactionary, and each left their own imprint on the town, but for Tone their sentiments were out of date, more in tune with Lord Charlemont's famous reluctance to touch the Catholic question back in the 1780s. Russell had informed his great friend of their opposition and, as we have seen, their position was rebutted skilfully in Tone's *Argument*.

During his first visit to Belfast in 1791, Tone recorded in his journal an 'amazing battle over dinner' on the Catholic issue on 21 October at Joy's house. Tone referred to Joy continuing to probe into issues that Tone felt he had already addressed in his pamphlet. Joy was, he said, 'an artful and troublesome antagonist', who agreed with the principle of liberating Catholics but baulked at the expediency. The following day, more arguments took place at the home of James Ferguson, another member of the Whig Club. Bruce, Halliday and Cunningham were there; 'Halliday pleasant—everyone else stupid', according to Tone. On the 25th there was another sparring match, this time at the home of Sam and Martha McTier, where Tone engaged in a two-hour debate with Waddell Cunningham, Robert Holmes and Bruce, the latter being, in Tone's words, 'an intolerant high priest'. Bruce set out his objections to Catholic rights at length and was supported by Cunningham, Thomas Greg, Robert Holmes and Henry Joy junior. Halliday was aware that the United Irish position had gained considerable traction in Belfast, such was the persuasiveness of Tone's pamphlet. Writing to his friend Lord Charlemont in November, the doctor noted that 'It is calculated to make, and has actually made here, a general impression in their favour. The gentleman himself passed a good many days among us lately and proselyted not a few.'

Opposition was demonstrated publicly in a town meeting in January 1792, during which Halliday declared that, while he supported the principle of Catholic rights, 'he thought they were not prepared for it, they must be farther enlightened and less under the dominion of the priesthood'. Tone was exasperated and observed wryly on his second visit to Belfast in July 1792 how 'the hair of Dr Halliday's wig miraculously grows grey with fear of the Catholics'. Waddell Cunningham was alarmed by Tone's renewed presence. On the eve of the third anniversary of the fall of the Bastille, Neilson uncovered a plot whereby Cunningham—his commanding officer in the First Volunteer Company—was attempting to force Volunteer officers from beyond Belfast into voting down the pro-Catholic resolution in the Bastille Day celebrations. Referring to Cunningham in his journal as 'a lying old scoundrel', Tone predicted hot work the next day. In the end, the resolutions were carried as the moderates lost the debate, with only Joy, Cunningham and three others opposing the resolutions.

Unwittingly, the cautious arguments of his rivals presented Tone with the type of challenge he relished throughout his career, allowing him to outmanoeuvre them with his writing and his personal charisma. That Tone and his allies carried the argument resulted not only from the strength of his debating skills but also from the briefings and pre-emptive discussions that enabled him to disarm the opposition in advance. Tone was a willing learner, always

> ' ... the United Irish position had gained considerable traction in Belfast, such was the persuasiveness of Tone's pamphlet.'

prepared to listen, embrace or, indeed, reject the analyses of others. His thinking developed continuously, and his political trajectory was shaped by his own analysis of situations, by external circumstances (such as the outbreak of war with France in February 1793) and by the dashed hopes of reform following the recall of Viceroy Fitzwilliam in 1795. Other factors, such as the nuanced and regional influences emanating from Belfast, played their part in forming his political life and legacy. Certainly, Tone both embraced and contributed to the radical sentiments in the town and was grateful for the input of his like-minded friends. Nevertheless, it was those often considered to be the anti-heroes of radical Belfast politics—Joy, Bruce, Cunningham and others—who brought out the best in Tone and pushed him the hardest to make an intellectual case for radical change.

- *Kenneth L. Dawson is a recently retired teacher and vice-principal.*

FURTHER READING

K.L. Dawson, *The Belfast Jacobin: Samuel Neilson and the United Irishmen* (Newbridge, 2017).

J. Quinn, *Soul on fire: a life of Thomas Russell* (Dublin, 2002).

F. Whelan, *May tyrants tremble: the life of William Drennan, 1754–1820* (Newbridge, 2020).

C.J. Woods (ed.), *Journals and memoirs of Thomas Russell* (Dublin, 1991).

William Drennan—both he and Tone have a claim to be the leading writer in the United Irish cause. (National Museums NI)

'REPUBLICANS AND SINNERS'— WOLFE TONE AND WILLIAM DRENNAN

BY **FERGUS WHELAN**

'REPUBLICANS AND SINNERS'—WOLFE TONE AND WILLIAM DRENNAN

BOTH THEOBALD WOLFE TONE and William Drennan have a claim to be the leading writer in the United Irish cause. Belfast-born Drennan relocated from Newry to Dublin in late 1789. He and Tone became acquainted in the winter of the following year, when Tone set up a short-lived political club with a few friends from his Trinity days and invited Drennan to become involved. Drennan was eight years Tone's senior and the two men had very different personalities. Tone was warm, generous and gregarious, unlike Drennan, who could be cold and off-putting. Yet it is said that within a short time, other than Thomas Russell, Tone's closest friend, Drennan had the most influence over him.

MUTUAL REGARD

From the beginning both men held each other in mutual regard, respect and admiration. Despite their contrasting personalities and some strains and disagreements, they always maintained this common

> ' ... a solemn declaration that committed every new member to building a brotherhood of affection among Irishmen of all religious persuasions.'

explicit esteem. Drennan complimented Tone for having a ready and excellent pen, while Tone tells us that most of the early publications of the United society were written by Drennan and were admirably well done.

Tone and Russell attended the founding meeting of the Belfast United Irishmen on 14 October 1791. They had met Sam McTier, Drennan's brother-in-law, the previous day and he told them of a secret committee which Tone believed 'directed the movements of Belfast'. Six months earlier, in May 1791, Drennan had written to Sam telling him that he was considering establishing a brotherhood of dedicated republicans in Dublin. Sam had shown Drennan's letter to leading Belfast radicals and assured him that 'if your club brotherhood takes place, we will immediately follow your example'. In the event, the Belfast people were ahead of Dublin in establishing the United Irish society.

The Dublin society was formed on 9 November 1791, when Drennan, James Napper Tandy and sixteen others came together at the Eagle tavern, Eustace Street, and adopted the resolutions that Tone and Russell had brought from the Belfast meeting. The Dublin group also adopted a test, which Drennan had prepared in advance. This test was in the form of a solemn declaration that committed every new member to building a brotherhood of affection among Irishmen of all religious persuasions. Tone and Russell were not present at the first Dublin meeting but were balloted into the club in their absence.

There was an early difference of opinion when Tone and Russell learned of Drennan's test. They were opposed to it as being likely to exclude men who would otherwise join up. Tandy supported Drennan, and Tone and Russell were defeated on the question. Drennan observed to Sam that Tone and Russell were

> '... imprudent and had made themselves unpopular which was evident from their not being appointed to the correspondence Committee of twelve. My chief fault to them is them being too reserved to some who are entitled to confidence, and they tended to treat fellow members as instruments rather than partners.'

Drennan was proud of his test, which might account for this truculent remark. It is likely that Tone and Russell felt that the Dublin club should follow Belfast rather than be unilaterally introducing new rules. This early tiff did not damage their relationship with Drennan, for even as he reported on the matter to Sam, Drennan recognised that Tone and Russell 'were sincere and able and zealous.'

THE CATHOLIC CONVENTION AND THE UNITED IRISH SOCIETY

The major difference that surfaced between Drennan and Tone, which arose from the latter's role as secretary to the Catholic Convention, was of a different order of magnitude. The United Irishmen wished to be publicly seen to support the Convention. For tactical reasons, Tone and the Convention did not choose to acknowledge this support. On 3 December 1792 the trial of the king of France began in Paris. That same day the Catholic Convention convened in the Tailors' Guild Hall on Dublin's Back Lane. There were 233 delegates representing every county in Ireland and 40 towns. The Dublin authorities clearly viewed the Convention as a serious threat. Perhaps to intimidate the delegates, the artillery corps marched through the city from its base in Chapelizod to the Castle.

The Dublin and Belfast United Irishmen expressed their support for the Convention. The Belfast society sent a supporting letter, which the Convention neither acknowledged nor published. When a delegation of the Dublin society, which included Archibald Hamilton Rowan and James Napper Tandy, brought a supporting message to the Tailors' Hall, they were not admitted but confined to an antechamber. When Drennan asked about the Belfast paper he reported that 'Tone had like to have snapped off my nose'. Samuel Neilson was furious with Tone for not giving him and his Belfast friends daily reports of the doings of the Convention. 'You have for five days of the most interesting crisis, kept us, your constituents, in the dark. We shall never forgive you.'

Tone was secretary to the Convention and he and the other leaders were in a difficult position. Resenting the slights and attacks from Dublin Castle, the Convention was hatching a plan to appeal directly to the king over the heads of the Dublin administration. The prospects of any such appeal might be damaged if the Catholics were publicly associating with the United Irishmen. While

Tone and the more militant Catholic leaders were themselves United Irishmen, they also had to be conscious of their more conservative membership, many of whom Drennan believed viewed the United Irish society 'as republicans and sinners'.

Initially Drennan understood the dilemma and told Sam, 'The truth is that the Catholics have two strings to their bow, a part to treat with Government and part to ally with us, and if one string cracks, why try the other. This is good and perhaps fair archery.' Two days after he wrote these words, however, the situation altered considerably. The government issued a proclamation effectively banning the Volunteers and threatening to disperse any corps that attempted to assemble.

Drennan and Rowan wanted a strong and spirited response to be made to show that the society had not been cowed. Drennan wrote and Rowan distributed *An address to the Volunteers*, which began with the French-sounding phrase 'Citizen Soldiers to Arms'. This led to the prosecution of both men for sedition.

In the run-up to the Convention, at the urging of the leading Catholics, Rowan and Tandy had been enrolling a new Volunteer corps with uniforms said to resemble those of the French National Guard. In its proclamation the grand jury referred to this new corps as 'involved in seditious meetings and being raised with devices against the constitution'. Tone and the Catholic leaders, however, were about to embark for London in the hope of meeting King George. They knew that they would not be granted a meeting if they publicly associated with those who were known to support the French Revolution when the king of France was on trial for his life.

When the proclamation against the Volunteers was published, the Catholics, who according to Drennan had first originated the idea of the corps, were now afraid and would have prevented any meeting of Volunteers. By 'damping' the new Volunteers, the Catholics were in Drennan's view leaving Rowan and Tandy in the lurch. In January 1793, when Rowan finally succeeded in getting a private meeting of the Volunteers, he suggested that they defy the proclamation and march out as soon as possible. He got no support from Tone, Russell and Thomas Addis Emmet, who in Drennan's view were 'so entwined with Catholic trammels [they] cannot go where their hearts lead them'. Drennan told his sister Martha:

'I feel a repulsion not an envy of Tone, though I agreed with all his principles before he became an [Catholic] agent, now Keogh guides him and both are artful men, very capable but such as you feel an unaccountable repugnance to.'

Tone and the Catholic delegates did meet the king, who, without committing either government, assured them that measures would be taken for their further relief. There followed negotiations with the Dublin administration, which resulted in substantial concessions in terms of the franchise, entry to Trinity College and military commissions but fell short on the key question of the right of Catholics to sit in parliament. In the aftermath of the partial relief of the resulting 1793 act, 'the Catholic Committee tore itself apart in mutual recrimination'. In April 1793 the Committee voted itself out of existence but awarded £1,500 to Tone for his services. Drennan thought this a handsome sum and believed it was well deserved.

THE JACKSON AFFAIR
In April 1794, as Archibald Hamilton Rowan was serving a two-year sentence for distributing Drennan's *Address to the Volunteers*, he was visited in his Newgate cell by Revd William Jackson, an Irish-born Anglican clergyman. Jackson was an agent of revolutionary France. Rowan, Jackson, Tone and Dr James Reynolds had a consultation, which resulted in Tone drawing up a document that could have exposed them to charges of treason. All were imperilled when this document fell into the hands of the government.

Above: Drennan's sister, Martha, with whom he corresponded over the years. (National Museums NI)

Rowan believed that his best chance to avoid the gallows was to escape from Newgate. When he broke out on 1 May a reward of £1,000 was offered for his recapture. Drennan stated that Rowan should die rather than be dragged back to jail. He hoped that Rowan had the courage to do so, for if not 'all the patriots are down'. Therefore his suicide was a matter of honour. Not to have the courage to do it would bring dishonour on all his associates and the United Irish Society. As Rowan fled, his friends suggested that he take two pistols with him, but he elected only to take a razor, as he had made up his mind not to be taken alive. The fact that Rowan recorded this in a memoir written for his children indicates that he regarded suicide in such a circumstance as wholly honourable.

In June 1794, grand jury bills of indictment for high treason were brought against the prisoner Revd William Jackson, the fugitive Rowan, Dr James Reynolds and Tone. Rowan had fled the prison and the country. Reynolds had made off to the United States. Drennan said that he wished with all his heart that Tone was with Reynolds.

In July Drennan was shown Jackson's indictment, which mentioned Tone as being seduced to write etc., etc. As no prosecution was

'REPUBLICANS AND SINNERS'—WOLFE TONE AND WILLIAM DRENNAN

brought against Tone, Drennan believed that he had entered 'an honourable compromise with government … He will not give evidence against any man which saves his own honour. He will not be prosecuted and probably get good recommendations for India.' Tone was still walking the streets of Dublin. Drennan, although he did not know the details, was sure that he had through some negotiation made a deal, which Drennan had no doubt was honourable on Tone's part. 'He would have suffered himself rather than give evidence against any unfortunate man …. As he stays here notwithstanding, he has certainly triumphed.'

In April 1795, when William Jackson appeared in the dock for sentence, he took his own life by ingesting poison:

'He beckoned to his counsel to approach him … and uttered in a whisper, and with a smile of mournful triumph … "We have deceived the senate".'

In those days suicide was generally regarded as shameful, but apparently not in this case. Although Jackson was a stranger in Dublin, Jonah Barrington tells us that his funeral to St Michan's was a splendid affair, attended by many lawyers and members of parliament. These 'respectable' men of Dublin were identifying with a man they did not know who had been convicted of treason and taken his own life. Drennan saluted Jackson's action, saying that 'he died like a Roman or should I say a Frenchman'. Tone's son William said of the manner of Jackson's death that 'It nobly redeemed his previous errors.'

TONE DEPARTS
After Jackson's trial, Tone partially fulfilled his side of the bargain with the government. He left Ireland for America via Belfast. He was not seen in Ireland again until October 1798, when he was taken prisoner in Lough Swilly. On 8 November Drennan told Martha, 'I hear Tone came into this city today under a strong military guard, dressed in rich French regimentals, and the carriage passed the Four Courts just as the lawyers were coming out. It is said he looked well and unembarrassed.' Later that month, when Drennan heard of Tone's death by his own hand, he told Martha, 'Tone is liberated'.

- *Fergus Whelan is the author of* May tyrants tremble: the life of William Drennan *(Irish Academic Press, 2020).*

FURTHER READING
M. Elliot, *Wolfe Tone: prophet of Irish independence* (Yale, 1989).
R.R. Madden, *The United Irishmen, their lives and times* (7 vols) (1842–60).

Below: 'MAY—EVENING SPORTS; or, ROWAN lost in the SMOKE'—a cartoon satirising Archibald Hamilton Rowan's escape from Newgate jail in May 1794. (*Faulkner's Weekly Magazine*, May 1794/NLI)

HOW RADICAL WAS WOLFE TONE?

BY **TIMOTHY MURTAGH**

Above: A miniature of Tone painted by his granddaughter, Mrs Tone Sampson. (Kay Dickason)

THEOBALD WOLFE TONE has commonly been described as the 'father' of Irish republicanism. Much like the debates surrounding the 'founding fathers' of the United States, however, how to characterise Tone's thoughts and beliefs has long been a subject of contention. While traditional accounts drew a straight line between Tone and later generations of Irish nationalists, starting in the 1970s, revisionist historians began to question whether he could be characterised in other terms: as an 'adventurer' or 'colonial outsider', or even as a 'frustrated imperialist'. Part of these debates was the question of Tone's status as a 'radical'. While there are multiple definitions of 'radicalism', in the eighteenth-century context it is commonly understood to include the extension of the franchise, the encouragement of popular participation in politics and the granting of universal civil liberties. Taking this description, Tone's reputation seems secure: he supported parliamentary reform and universal manhood suffrage (votes for women would not emerge as a mainstay of radical politics until much later). It is the social and economic dimension of Tone's thought that has continued to be most controversial, however. Tone may have believed in expanding political rights, but what about economic rights? Did he believe in State intervention to alleviate poverty or to provide basic measures of welfare? What did Tone think about collective action among workers or the nature of property relations? During the twentieth century, left-wing writers such as T.A. Jackson, Erich Strauss and Seán Cronin emphasised Tone's social radicalism. During the 1960s and '70s some even sought to characterise him as a 'proto-socialist', with left-republicans such as Tomás Mac Giolla and Cathal Goulding seeking to analyse Tone's writings from an explicitly Marxist perspective. Developing arguments first laid out by James Connolly, others have argued that Tone's politics were based on the same values as later labour and socialist movements.

Below: A poster advertising the 1973 Wolfe Tone Bodenstown commemoration of the Official Republican Movement. Left-republicans such as Tomás Mac Giolla sought to analyse Tone's writings from an explicitly Marxist perspective. But how credible are such arguments? (An Coiste Cuimhneachain Naisiunta)

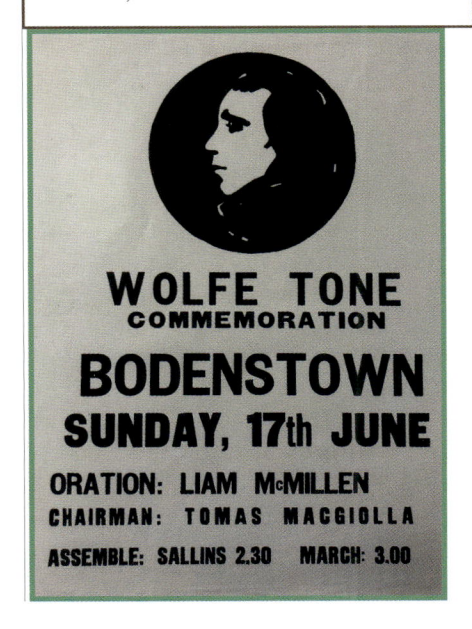

How radical was Wolfe Tone?

Above: Whitley Stokes—one of several prominent members of the Dublin Society of United Irishmen who in 1794 opposed universal suffrage. Tone vocally disagreed with such arguments. (NLI)

TONE'S SOCIAL PREJUDICES

How credible are such arguments? We might begin by looking at Tone's own social background. Born the son of a prosperous coach-maker, he received an élite education at Trinity College, Dublin, and London's Middle Temple. He soon discovered, however, that the life of a young barrister was economically precarious and, despite a short period of patronage by élite Irish Whig politicians, his career opportunities were limited by the entrenched power of the Ascendancy. To Marxist historians of eighteenth-century revolutions this all looks very familiar: a frustrated and articulate member of the 'middling sorts', alienated by a privileged aristocracy. In this interpretation, Tone would not have been out of place in the Boston of John Adams or the Paris of Abbé Sieyès, with all the potential limitations of such 'bourgeois revolutionaries'. Advocating an extension of political rights, such men were fearful of the popular classes, worried that a rhetoric of 'equality' might be taken much further by the 'lower orders', eventually threatening conventional property rights. Can this description be applied to Theobald Wolfe Tone?

Hostile commentators have frequently alighted on comments made by Tone that seem to express snobbery or contempt for the 'lower orders'. Some examples include his harsh comparison between the 'mob' in France and in Ireland ('Our mob, very shabby fellows'), or his comments on the propensity of Irishmen to alcoholism ('the devil of it is that poor Pat is a little given to drink'). During his time in America, Tone reserved his toughest verdict for Irish immigrants in Pennsylvania: 'if you meet a confirmed blackguard you may be sure he is Irish; you will, of course, observe I speak of the lower

> **'... a frustrated and articulate member of the 'middling sorts', alienated by a privileged aristocracy?'**

orders. They are as boorish and ignorant as the Germans, as uncivil and uncouth as the Quakers, and as they have ten times more animal spirits than both, they are much more actively troublesome.' He qualified this statement, however, by attributing the Irish character to being 'corrupted by their own execrable government at home'. Traces of élitism can even be found in Tone's most famous publication, *An argument on behalf of the Catholics of Ireland*, where he criticises poorer Protestants who possessed the vote, terming them 'the wretched tribe of forty-shilling freeholders'. He described how they were 'driven to their octennial market by their landlords, as much their property as the sheep or the bullocks which they brand with their names', calling them 'a disgrace to our constitution and country'.

Yet such remarks are hardly a 'smoking gun'. Tone's comments on the forty-shilling freeholders were made strategically, in a pamphlet aimed at winning over nervous and moderate Protestants. His criticism of the forty-shilling franchise was more a criticism of the way landlords manipulated the electoral system than a condemnation of mass democracy. His private comments and journal entries must be treated even more carefully. Tone often put pen to paper without reserve, and his more impulsive comments are easy fodder for selective quotation. Tone's statements, whether private or public, must also be considered within the wider context of the United Irish movement. Looking at the social views of his contemporaries, it becomes clear that Tone was firmly within the progressive wing of the United Irishmen.

A RANGE OF POLITICAL OUTLOOKS IN THE UNITED IRISHMEN

During its early phase, the United Irishmen contained members with a range of political outlooks. Many who joined in the early years of the society did not consider themselves as French-style 'Jacobins' or republicans but as moderates who hoped to bring about enough modest reform to *prevent* a popular revolution. Many United Irishmen were particularly sensitive to accusations that they were 'levellers' or anarchists who invited mob rule. In 1792 they had felt the need to state explicitly that 'by liberty we never understood unlimited freedom, nor by equality the levelling of property or the destruction of subordination'. That same year the *Northern Star*, the United Irish newspaper in Belfast, strongly supported a local company of Volunteers who suppressed protests by weavers seeking higher wages. The paper ran editorials critical of journeymen and tradesmen who formed 'combinations' (early trade unions), portraying striking workers as a threat to Belfast's economy and good order. The following year, the Dublin Society of United Irishmen refused to respond to an address brought to them by local weavers owing to the fear that the society's enemies 'would say that we were reduced to the necessity of corresponding with a mob'. This was perhaps unsurprising: at this time the Dublin Society included members who were employers with a history of confronting organised labour, several having been engaged in disputes with their journeymen.

Furthermore, not every member of the United Irishmen supported giving political rights to those without substantial property. In 1794 the Dublin Society had only narrowly voted to reject property qualifications as a condition for the franchise in its proposals, with the committee in charge of preparing the plan voting 11–9. Several prominent members, such as William Drennan, John Chambers and Whitley Stokes, had strongly disagreed with the idea of universal suffrage, sympathising with more moderate reformers like Henry Grattan, who warned that 'if you transfer the power of the state to those who have nothing in the country, they will afterwards transfer the property'. Whitley Stokes even went as far as to publish his own reform plans, which included property qualifications as 'Liberty is only a good as the means of virtue and happiness, and more may be lost than these than gained in the point of liberty by the voting of the very lowest class'.

LABOUR AS PROPERTY

It is significant that Tone vocally disagreed with such arguments; he was a firm supporter of granting universal manhood suffrage, without any property qualification. The United Irish plan for reform that was published in 1794 (with Tone's support) not only called for universal manhood suffrage but also put forward a creative argument that justified the political participation of the working classes. It argued that, even if political rights flowed from the possession of property, it was possible to apply an interpretation that redefined property to incorporate the demands of labour: 'Property is merely the collection of labour … and scattered labour of the lowest rank is as real and ought to be as really represented as the most fixed and solid property … Giving political power exclusively to property collected, not to the mass of living labour, has been in all ages, and particularly in modern times, the true cause … of aristocratic despotism.' Significantly, this belief in universal political rights could co-exist with a disdain for labour organisations like the journeymen combinations in Dublin and Belfast. The United Irishmen believed that it was interference in the free market that hurt the working classes—such as government monopolies, tariffs, charters and guild regulations. From this perspective, journeymen combinations were simply a form of monopoly.

> **'Many United Irishmen were particularly sensitive to accusations that they were 'levellers' or anarchists who invited mob rule.'**

At the heart of the republican vision of the 1790s was the idea of a harmonious and class-free society. The existence of proto-trade unions and the beginning of class solidarity flew in the face of that vision. Few within the United Irish leadership foresaw how the unrestricted operation of the free market would not bring about a harmonious society of independent producers but would lead to wider inequalities, yet this should not detract from the fact that their endorsement of universal suffrage put the United Irishmen at the cutting edge of European reform movements.

TONE AS 'A LIBERTY WEAVER'

Meanwhile, a frequent criticism of the movement has been that, whatever their political aims, they lacked a coherent approach to social issues. Marianne Elliott once argued that despite the 'republicanization of their political aims there was no corresponding extension of their social programme … the Irish people might have considered the changes involved in a United Irish republic as little more than a palace revolution'. Needless to say, such views can be contested. The United Irishmen certainly put an emphasis on reforming parliament, but this was seen as just a starting-point. As they once proclaimed, 'with a parliament thus reformed everything is easy, without it nothing can be done'. In a 1794

HOW RADICAL WAS WOLFE TONE?

Above: Thomas Addis Emmet—when questioned in the aftermath of the 1798 Rebellion, he stated that, 'if a revolution ever takes place [in Ireland], a very different system of political economy will be established from what has hitherto prevailed here'. (Madden, *United Irishmen*/NLI)

address 'to the poorer classes of the community', they argued that 'poverty and wretchedness' could be redressed by a parliamentary reform that would give the poor their 'just proportion of influence in the legislature, and by such a measure only'. The United Irishmen believed that the economic grievances of the poor were created by the political system and therefore could only be rectified by reforming that system. One of the United Irish leaders, Thomas Addis Emmet, when questioned in the aftermath of the 1798 Rebellion, stated that 'if a revolution ever takes place [in Ireland], a very different system of political economy will be established from what has hitherto prevailed here'.

Exactly what this new 'system of political economy' would have looked like is uncertain. Some United Irishmen believed that Irish independence from Britain would unleash the country's potential as a centre for manufacturing and export. They similarly argued that the transformation of Ireland into a republic would ensure the end of government corruption and waste, with the various pensioners and courtiers no longer paid from the public purse. The resulting reduction in taxes would further stimulate the economy, raising many out of poverty. While this was undoubtedly an optimistic vision, it had a mass appeal. The language of 'commercial grievance' was a potent one, highlighting the ruinous economic effects of British political dominance over Ireland. Tone had pioneered this argument in 1793 in his pamphlet *To the manufacturers of Dublin*. In a carefully crafted piece of propaganda, Tone took on the persona of 'A Liberty Weaver', adopting a down-to-earth style and displaying familiarity with the deprivations of the city's manufacturers, depicting war as an instrument of the ruling class to increase taxation and patronage. The pamphlet asked 'how many of our industrious people [the war] will drive to idleness and want and beggary; how much of our best blood it will spill; and how little of our wealth it will leave with us; and then, perhaps, they will begin to ask what is all this for?' Tone was also alive to the grievances of the rural, not just the urban, poor. In 1796, while in exile in France, he produced *An address to the peasantry of Ireland*, which advised the Irish rural poor what they had to gain from a revolution: lower taxes, the abolition of tithes and the resale of confiscated church lands. It was a vision that placed great emphasis on helping that 'numerous and useful body of the community who are, like yourselves, the tillers and cultivators of the earth, by whose labour all other classes are supported and sustained'.

'THE MEN OF NO PROPERTY'

In support of Tone's reputation as a social radical, left-wing republicans have frequently pointed to a diary entry made in April 1796:

> 'Our independence must be had at all hazards. If the men of property will not support us, they must fall. We can support ourselves by the aid of that numerous and respectable class of the community—the men of no property.'

Like many well-known aspects of the Irish nationalist tradition, this quote became the target of revisionist scholarship, which sought to locate Tone's use of the term 'property' in its eighteenth-century context, where 'property' was commonly taken to mean *landed* property (as opposed to commercial or financial wealth). In this reading, the 'men of no property' to whom Tone referred were the 'respectable' middle classes he had encountered in Dublin and Belfast—lawyers, merchants, doctors, textile manufacturers. Again, such verdicts can be questioned. Jim Smyth, who took the phrase 'men of no property' for his landmark study of popular radicalism, has argued that, whatever Tone's original meaning, his words have assumed a life and meaning beyond their author's intent. Even during Tone's lifetime such terms were open to interpretation. Would a struggling weaver or farm labourer in the 1790s not have considered himself a 'man of no property'?

Even accepting the social-radical interpretation of such statements, however, Tone's comments on issues like economic inequality are frustratingly thin, although we may infer something from his personal friendships. Tone was close to several figures who had a strong sympathy for the poor. One such man was Thomas Russell, whom Tone met in the gallery of the Irish parliament in 1790, quickly becoming fast friends. Tone's diaries are full of accounts of their travels together, their conversations and their occasional drinking binges. Russell lived a wandering and sometimes chaotic existence, but his empathy for the problems of the poor was unshakeable, even when this brought him into conflict with colleagues. Perhaps unique among the United Irishmen, Russell championed the rights of journeymen to form trade unions, arguing in their favour in the pages of the *Northern Star*. While Tone was impressed by mechanical inventions and the industrial growth of Belfast's new mills, Russell had the foresight to see some of the harmful effects on workers, including the detrimental effects of factory work and the potential abuse of female and child labour.

While Tone's diaries have been widely available in print since the 1820s, Russell's writings were for a long time inaccessible. Thanks, however, to the work of C.J. Woods, an edition of Russell's journals, now readily available, makes it clear just how crucial an influence he was on Tone. This even extended to cheering Tone up about the prospects of Irish independence. Russell recalled how Tone, at a low point in early 1794, lamented that there was 'nothing to be expected from this country except from the sans culottes who are too ignorant for any thinking man to wish to see in power'. Yet Russell did not share Tone's pessimism about Ireland's 'sans culottes', and over the next several years he helped push his friend in a more populist direction. It is perhaps telling that Tone's oft-quoted declaration concerning 'the men of no property' was foreshadowed by a diary entry that Russell made in July 1793, where he argued that, 'from what I can see, the men of property, whether landed or commercial, are decidedly against a struggle … The people are beginning to see this and in time when they will feel their strength and injuries they will do it themselves and adieu to property!' In his journals Russell denounced laws made by the rich that valued property more than human welfare and the common good, going so far as to declare that 'property must be altered in some measure'.

While evidence of Tone's social radicalism may be slight, his close friendship with Russell makes it difficult to conceive of him as a social conservative. To base Tone's social views on stray comments about the 'mob' is a flimsy argument. At the same time, it may not be accurate to describe Tone as a 'proto-socialist', simply because that term is too imprecise. The politics of the 1790s belonged to a different world than the type of industrial society that produced socialism. To ask whether Tone was a socialist is like asking whether Galileo was a quantum physicist; it is to apply an anachronism, which does more to mystify than clarify. If the views of men like Thomas Russell had been taken to their logical conclusion, they *might* have approached something like socialism, or at least advocacy for a strong welfare state. In an alternative reality, where United Irish attempts at revolution were successful, would Tone have sided with men like Russell, allying himself with the country's 'sans culottes'? As fun as it is to indulge in this type of hypothetical, it is impossible to know for sure. What one can say is that without Tone the development of Irish socialism and labour radicalism would have been very different. The United Irishmen pioneered an alliance between middle-class radicals and a popular base, helping to give the working classes a sense of political agency. This opened the door, allowing for socially radical interpretations of the republican project, even if they were at odds with some of its leaders. Tone's service to the political prospects of the working class should not be underestimated.

- *Timothy Murtagh is a research fellow with the Virtual Record Treasury of Ireland.*

FURTHER READING

R. Madden, *The United Irishmen, their lives and times* (7 vols) (1842–60).
T. Murtagh, *Irish artisans and radical politics 1776–1820* (Liverpool, 2023).
J. Quinn, 'The United Irishmen and social reform', *Irish Historical Studies* (November 1998).
J. Smyth, *The men of no property: Irish radicals and popular politics in the late eighteenth century* (London, 1992).
C.J. Woods (ed.), *Journals and memoirs of Thomas Russell* (Dublin, 1991).

> OUR INDEPENDENCE MUST BE HAD AT ALL HAZARDS IF THE MEN OF PROPERTY WILL NOT SUPPORT US THEY MUST FALL WE CAN SUPPORT OURSELVES BY THE AID OF THAT NUMEROUS AND RESPECTABLE CLASS OF THE COMMUNITY THE MEN OF NO PROPERTY
> — Theobald Wolfe Tone

Above: Tone's famous quote on display at Bodenstown. But what did he mean by 'the men of no property'?

Tone visited the Muséum Central des Arts (or Louvre, opened in 1793) twice in early March 1796, though the skylights in the Grande Galerie were added later. He commented that artists could copy the best works of the best masters. (RMN, Paris)

FEELINGS AND 'LITERARY FAME'?

BY **SYLVIE KLEINMAN**

TONE'S SELF-WRITINGS
AND THE READER EXPERIENCE

FOR ERNIE O'MALLEY, heroes were 'abstractions', read about in school only in relation to events and who had nothing to do with living. In his memoir *On another man's wound* (1936), he described finding Theobald Wolfe Tone's *Autobiography* at home, embedding that canonical text of Irish rebel self-writing in the one that he was creating. Its pages were uncut, and O'Malley read slowly: Tone had been the first to unite Catholics and Presbyterians 'in the national effort'.

THE 'VERY CHOICEST READING'

Tone's full public and private writings were first published by his son William as the *Life* in 1826, an edition spanning c. 1,000 pages and avidly read. Even those rejecting his 1790s militant separatism and revolutionary republicanism became captivated by 'Wolfe Tone': a 'most extraordinary man', whose 'history' was the 'most curious' of the times in which he lived. The Duke of Wellington was overheard saying this as early as 1831; few books had interested him as much as Tone's 'journal', according to chatter relayed by Thomas Moore. During the Irish history wars triggered by the first Home Rule Bill, the MP George Trevelyan (son of Sir Charles) enthusiastically replied in 1886 to a suggested list of the best hundred Irish books: he only read for pleasure, and agreed that the '*Autobiography* of Wolfe Tone' was among the 'very choicest reading'.

By 1827 an abridged edition of

44 /WOLFE TONE 225

the *Life* had omitted the pamphlets, and an 1828 pocket-size *Life … written by himself* only reprinted the autobiography and extracts from the French diary, in 347 pages. A copy of it read by Casement in prison was gifted to the National Library of Ireland. These two key texts sufficed, and through them Tone's interior voice entered the public consciousness. As some editions only printed the French diary, this elevated his mission to France for Ireland's sovereignty to a romantic hero-quest, framed in his own words. Many episodes, like meeting 'Buonaparte', were easily reimagined. First-person narratives had become popular in Tone's time, and during the 1820s a wealth of memoirs appeared, by both soldiers and civilians. Publishers knew that self-written portrayals of character sold well.

Because of the misleading titles, Tone's memoir and diary are often conflated; despite overlapping features, their styles differ. Both yielded iconic pronouncements by Tone on a sovereign and democratic Ireland which became ubiquitous nationalist references. In 1914 Pearse explicitly referred to Tone's *Autobiography* as the 'first gospel of the New Testament of Irish nationality'. This exalted biblical allusion, inherited from the Fenians, had also been voiced during his seminal Ciceronian graveside oration at Bodenstown in 1913. Pearse had praised Tone's noble spirit, which 'laughed and sang with the gladness of a boy'. Sometimes a 'gust of passionate love' for his wife and children would break into what he 'was writing or saying: "O my babies, my babies", he exclaims', said Pearse. Marianne Elliot opens her biography of Tone by stressing that the 'spontaneity, humour and openness' of the diary made him 'one of the most accessible' and familiar of historical figures. Yet conventional historical narrative has not sufficiently linked Tone's Enlightenment sentimentalism and belief in man's capacity for action to his political energies. Let us finally understand and value how this quality, conveyed through his formidable writing talent which even Leonard MacNally had praised, so connected him with readers.

Above: 'To Mrs Martin I am indebted …'—Tone had performed in John Home's *Douglas* in the Kirwan's Lane Theatre, Galway, on 8 August 1783 with Richard and Elizabeth Martin. This review is the earliest extant document in his hand. (NLI)

AUTOBIOGRAPHY

The conventional explanation for Tone's starting his autobiography in Paris (August 1796) flows from his own words. His diary for the preceding days bristles with anxiety, energetic frustration and annoyance. Interminable delays prevented his departure to join the expedition to Ireland and strike for her freedom: 'Blank! Terrible, terrible! I fret myself absolutely sick these days.' Now it was another eleven days: 'Damn it! … How shall I get over them?' William observed that his father's pen 'flowed with light and easy grace' and was 'allowed to run in these careless' jottings. Regardless of their political sympathies, future readers empathised with Tone's straightforward yet eloquent expressions of mood: 'I am weary of complaining that I am weary'.

The autobiography, supposedly written 'to fill a vacant hour' or several, is consistently serious, unlike the bouncy and meditative diary. There may be echoes of Rousseau's *Confessions*, but Tone does not atone in his 'memorandums on my life and opinions'. As in the diary, but more formally, he forcefully projects his character and motivations onto readers, whether they would later regard him as a scoundrel and traitor or as the political saint he never envisioned himself to be. A rare sentimental aside in the memoir leads to a defining thread, overlooked by the fact that he intended it mainly, as Elliott puts it, as a '*political* testimonial for posterity' (my emphasis). Bluntly aware that he may never see them again, Tone wrote about a handful of 'inestimable friends' (apart from his closest, Thomas Russell). Exiled as he was, it was a 'consolation' to his soul to 'dwell upon their merits'. He then apologised for 'this long digression' in which he (unapologetically) had 'dealt with affection'. Readers could vividly sense emotions stirred in the very act of writing. Then he returned to 'my history', a recurring frame in both texts, which projects a vision never properly discussed. Recalling his time in London writing book reviews, he also made a compelling statement: 'as to literary fame, I had then no great ambition to obtain it'. So did he *now*, writing his autobiography? He tracked how he became 'a sort of political character' after his first pamphlet, then 'pretty notorious' after openly hinting at separatism in the next one, foregrounding writing in his career. His biographer identifies a 'sense of destiny' in the autobiography, which apparently is 'not present' in the journals that followed. This merits revisiting.

ACCIDENTAL TOURIST
Tone ended his autobiography when his French mission began, alerting anticipated readers that his 'adventures' were 'fully detailed in the diary' regularly kept since his arrival. His journals thus generally became a parallel autobiographical narrative linked to his memoir, and he had clearly agreed with his wife Matilda that they would eventually become what we call an open source. In 1814 she privately stated that his papers would 'certainly appear', but not till they became 'purely historical'. The memoir was supposedly written for his sons, should it fall into their hands 'hereafter', but, unlike the vivacious diary, it had little to engage the imagination of very young children. O'Malley had been specific when stressing that Tone had been the 'first human note' among historical heroes. '"Drunk again" in his diary meant much', O'Malley wrote: 'it brought him down to mortal level'. Yet Tone was mostly soberly goal-oriented when lobbying in France 'to overthrow the British government in Ireland', as Wellington put it. His mission transformed him into an accidental tourist, on a privileged Grand Tour in wartime that he had only read about, and his powers of description are mighty.

Readers were swept along in his journey of discovering Paris, republican society and ceremonial in France,

> **'Readers were swept along in his journey of discovering Paris, republican society and ceremonial in France ... '**

followed him into the chambers of official decision-making, then became complicit in his nightly debriefings. It is little wonder that Thomas Davis imagined himself in Tone's study, watching him write at his desk strewn with military plans and memorials. The diary became an exceptional historical source, as he recorded every 'material' and 'minute' detail for Matilda, then in America. He even historicised starting this 'practice' in his memoir during his first, and truly historical, journey to Belfast in 1791. He had then reassured 'Matty' (Matilda) in a letter that he 'journalised everything', while bragging that his diary was 'wittier than Swift's'. In France in 1796 he wrote that she would consider even 'trifling' circumstances 'of consequence', but his private musings became intermingled with military strategy, revolutionary ideology, cultural commentary and more.

LONELINESS
A compelling dimension of the Paris diary, vigorously bouncing off the page for about eight months until he left for his military posting, is his intense emotional loneliness. Innumerable cries of despair longed for Russell's company and advice. Endless waiting meant that his 'mind was overgrown with docks and thistles'. He was 'puzzled in mazes and perplexed in errors', here paraphrasing Joseph Addison's *Cato* (1712), one of the innumerable quotes from his vast reading. One summer day he 'scaled Montmartre' '*all alone*', he emphasised by underlining in the manuscript. It was 'terrible' to have nobody to 'communicate the million of observations which *"rise and shine, evaporate and fall"* in my mind' (from Samuel Johnson's *Vanity of human wishes* (1749)). Living through a form of lockdown with no communication whatsoever, Tone perceived the psychological weight of having no one with whom to share his opinions. This transformed his journalising into a running human conversation, often deeply melancholic, and later a stirring read. He usually exuberantly bounced back: his favourite optimistic motto, '*Nil Desperandum!*', peppers his diary, and he treasured the exclamation mark. His writerly self-awareness comes across, as when he verbalised the process as therapeutic, as if he were assessing a blog today: 'when I begin to write these ingenious memorandums, I feel just as if I were chatting with my dearest Love, and I know not when to leave off'. Tom Bartlett stressed this quality of immediacy and cited Tone's own description of the journal as 'a faithful transcription of all that passes in my mind', 'my hopes and fears … doubts and expectations' about his mission. These frequent polarities also display his artful choice of words and lyrical way of stringing them together. For a historian, the assumption that such a subjective source is also factually true is essential, but to a wider audience Tone's eloquent and persuasive writing simply made it credible. He drew others into his private introspection, and, lightly applying some much-needed literary theory, Declan Kiberd has observed how Tone created a space and role for the reader. 'Trifling' as his memorandums were, they became 'a great resource to me', and eventually would resonate with others.

'TO THE MOMENT'
Tone precisely echoed how literary theory defines Samuel Richardson's seminal technique of writing 'to the moment' in Enlightenment novels. Readers relate immediately to a character whose letter to someone they are reading. Tone preferred to write quickly after events: 'The only good in my journals is that they are written at *the moment* and represent things exactly as they strike me' (my

Below: As in this 1822 painting by George Arnald (1763–1841), Montmartre was still a rural village when Tone was there on 9 July 1796. His diary for that day states that he 'had a magnificent view of Paris at my feet'. (Musée Carnavalet)

FEELINGS AND 'LITERARY FAME'? TONE'S SELF-WRITINGS AND THE READER EXPERIENCE

emphasis). He voiced how the black-out of news from Matty affected him when he learned that a letter privately conveyed from America had arrived. 'My heart is up in my mouth! I am in a frenzy till I get my letter. I have not had one line … in six months. How is my dearest life and soul, and our darling little babies?', the 'Daffs'. They would eventually be reunited in May 1797, after sixteen months, but he often pondered that this was only possible if they faced the perils of the ocean. Barely a few days in France, he heard of a tragic shipwreck within yards of the coast. A mother had perished 'with her infants. It is too horrible to think of. Oh my babies, my babies, if your little bodies were sunk in the ocean what should I do?' It was fashionable for a time to belittle Pearse. Yet he was anything but deluded when referring to Tone speaking from beyond the grave in and from his diary, the other 'gospel'.

Tone's self-perception as an agent of historical change permeates his early French diary. Deconstructing strengths and weaknesses of a day's discussions, he amused himself that there could be a lot of 'vanity' in an entry, but after barely three weeks a role for him as an official representative of the new Ireland in France had been outlined. This made his memorandums very wise, 'for a minister plenipotentiary planning a revolution', and as an 'ambassador incognito', navigating the 'wheels within wheels' of French politics, he could pat himself on the back with giddiness: '*And now* am I not a pretty fellow to go to the Directory?' He frequently wrote the reader into his wily negotiating stratagems, signalling asides in accounts of discussions. After privately disagreeing with Minister Delacroix about invasion tactics, he added in the diary, as if whispering, 'In this Delacroix is mistaken'. Further down, he recorded something he uttered, but then wrote 'N.B. In this I lied a little'. Yet this avowal made him truthful. That the claret often flowed is not silenced, which may explain some microtheatricals. An administrative 'blunder' had led to a police com-

Above: Maria Tone, who signed herself 'M. Smith', Tone's pseudonym at the time, had just turned eleven when she wrote this letter to her father c. 14 June 1797. She was then living with her mother and brothers William (1791–1828) and Francis (1793–1806) in Nanterre, west of Paris. She died in March 1803. (Katherine Prendergast/TCD)

missioner knocking on the door of his lodgings to haul him away as an illegal alien. Tone dramatised the encounter thus: '*I jumped suddenly upon him and deprived him of the use of his weapon* … producing my permission to remain'. That he had often contemplated his likely fate should they land in Ireland is not sufficiently stressed in the debate about how he died. He couldn't help 'laughing at my own wit, or rather Sheridan's', after quoting from his hit comedy *The Rivals*: 'Oh … that I could be shot before I was aware!' Indeed, he might have the 'good fortune to be killed in action' in a sea battle, rather than be 'hanged as a traitor and embowelled' on Irish soil. These last words were written in December 1796, on a storm-tossed ship within sight of the Bantry coast. He closed that year's diary by concluding that it had 'been a very remarkable one in my history', which it certainly had. Tone's appeal, however, lies well beyond the sphere of political history.

LETTER FROM HIS DAUGHTER
In the only surviving letter to Tone from his daughter Maria, she wrote eloquently and explained that she had not yet started to write an account of her travels. So apparently her 'Fadoff' (father) had encouraged her to do so, a welcome corrobor-

ation of international scholarship on the Enlightenment mind-set of nurturing observation in a child. At any age, reflecting on new experiences and the sensations they triggered and capturing this on paper was part of being. Maria enjoyed reading his journals with her mother as he travelled with the French army, filling more notebooks. In playful family letters Tone challenged his precocious daughter with his favoured literary quotation game, many 'stolen from Shakespeare', and they contain candid expressions of love between him, 'our dear Matty' and 'the Daffs'. Pearse had stirred that gathering at Bodenstown with those insights: 'it was the memory of such love as this, with the little hands of his children plucking at his heartstrings, that he lay down to die' in that Dublin prison cell. If Pearse's propagandist style is seen as excessive, it is because the so-called discovery during the Decade of Centenaries that Ireland possessed a history of emotion is misguided. It has always been there, but much of the writing on Tone and 1798 pre-dates so-called interdisciplinary perspectives and did not engage with the sensibility and *mentalités* of his times, to which our current age of mindfulness can relate. History writing in the 1970s and '80s, like Irish society, was somewhat frightened of character, not to mention ambition, and was not ready to deconstruct nineteenth-century heroisation. Much had been left to 'literary' or 'cultural' scholars, e.g. insightful travel accounts.

We now know that Tone had been writing, and quite sentimentally, since the age of twenty. His infatuation for Mrs Elizabeth Martin was captured in a gushing review of a play in which he had acted alongside her and her husband. It ended with him admitting that 'what I felt I wrote, and I wrote it as I felt it'. Years later that technique would be applied with greater maturity to create one of the most influential written artefacts of Ireland. Writing his autobiography later exposed him, Marianne Elliott observed, to accusations that he was creating his 'own myth for posterity'. This made sense in the context of the cult of 'Wolfe' Tone in the 1980s, but Tone never formulated a vision even hinting at the mythical. Close reading shows that his sense of destiny does permeate the French diary, but who would deny that he had 'a pretty serious business' on his hands? On his 33rd birthday in France, he mused with gravity that Alexander the Great at that age had conquered the world, though he elsewhere joked about comparing himself to such a great man. He would 'push everything as far as he could' for the 'liberty and independence of my country', the safety of his family and 'last, I hope, a well-earned reputation'. But he lived in an age when

Above: On his 33rd birthday, 20 June 1796, Tone wrote this diary entry and reflected that, if his mission in Paris succeeded, 'I may make some noise in the world yet', and that he hoped to someday achieve 'a well-earned reputation'. (TCD)

HISTORY IRELAND/ 49

men rose from obscurity to become reputable, and he had 'a violent objection' to perhaps being hanged as a traitor in Ireland. In what Guy Beiner may call an act of pre-memory, Tone had written his autobiography to pre-empt oblivion or, worse, being remembered dishonourably as a scoundrel in the 'hereafter'. Both of Tone's first-person writings assert what we recognise today as self-belief in the face of great challenges.

At an early stage of the French mission, Tone's 'men of no property' statement ended a multi-layered diary entry, and its misinterpretation as plucked from its original context has been well elucidated by Jim Smyth. John Mitchel had made it iconic by citing it on the masthead of his short-lived and inflammatory *United Irishman* newspaper in 1848, renewing Tone's mission to achieve Ireland's 'independence … at all hazards'. His writings were increasingly regarded as an authoritative source of rebel history, and Mitchel's use of it was even read out in the House of Lords but with no need to condemn the original author—he had paid the ultimate price. In the diary the 'men of no property' was preceded by a flash of black humour about landing in Ireland. Quoting from Smollett's picaresque *Humphrey Clinker*, Tone hoped that 'Please God, the dogs shall not have my poor blood to lick'. In his pre-Castle days, Augustine Birrell deemed his account 'stirring' and proclaimed him a 'true humourist'. Safe in his Berlin hotel in 1915, Joseph Mary Plunkett had relieved anxiety in his own diary while recalling a tricky moment at the Swiss border. An officious official had queried his papers, but he had '*jumped suddenly upon him*' to deprive '*him of the use of his weapon*'! Tone's *Autobiography* had been Plunkett's 'bible', as his sister Geraldine had relayed to future generations. It is time we appreciated how Tone's masterful skill when writing his Enlightenment testaments to life, family and fatherland created an unrivalled and immersive reader experience, which underpinned his posthumous cult and won the gamble to 'make some noise in the world'.

'Please God, the dogs shall not have my poor blood to lick.'

- *Sylvie Kleinman is Visiting Research Fellow at the Department of History, Trinity College, Dublin, and associate researcher, TCD Centre for the Book.*

FURTHER READING

T. Bartlett (ed.), *The life of Theobald Wolfe Tone* (Dublin, 1998).

D. Kiberd, 'Republican self-fashioning: the journal of Wolfe Tone', in O. Walsh (ed.), *Ireland abroad* (Dublin, 2003), 16–35.

S. Kleinman, 'Ambassador incognito and accidental tourist: cultural perspectives on Theobald Wolfe Tone's mission to France, 1796–8', *Journal of Irish and Scottish Studies* 2 (1) (2008), 101–22.

S. Kleinman, 'Matty and the Daffs: the family life of Theobald Wolfe Tone in exile (1795–1798)', in M. Hatfield, J. Kruse & R. Nic Congáil (eds), *Historical perspectives on parenthood and childhood in Ireland* (Galway, 2018), 23–43.

Below: Fête des Victoires—on 29 May 1796 Tone attended this 'superb spectacle' at the Champ de Mars (Paris) to honour France's military victories in Italy. He sat among the diplomatic corps 'at the foot of the altar' but 'chose to remain *incognito*'.

'ALL THE WORLD'S A STAGE'— THEOBALD WOLFE TONE AND SHAKESPEARE

BY **EILÍS SMYTH**

Above: William Shakespeare by John Taylor (*c.* 1610). In 1763, the year of Tone's birth, the Dublin public saw fifteen of Shakespeare's plays performed on at least 39 occasions. (NPG, London)

THEOBALD WOLFE TONE was born in 1763 in Dublin. The future United Irishman's birth took place three days after a performance of Shakespeare's comedy *As You Like It* and three days before a production of the first part of the historical epic *Henry IV*. Both productions were staged at the relatively new Crow Street theatre—about a ten-minute walk from Tone's birthplace—whose manager then possessed the city's royal theatre patent, previously held at the Smock Alley theatre on what is now Essex Street. Tone's Dublin was theatrically vibrant, and, like the eighteenth-century stages in London, the city's theatres paid their dues to William Shakespeare. In the year of Tone's birth, the Dublin public saw fifteen of Shakespeare's plays performed on at least 39 occasions. In 1763 the most popular plays were *Julius Caesar*, *The Merry Wives of Windsor*, *Othello* and *Henry IV, Part* One, highlighting a catholic taste for Shakespearean drama in the Dublin audience. The breadth and consistency of these performances is indicative of an established, century-long tradition of Shakespeare in the Irish capital.

SMOCK ALLEY
Built in 1662, Smock Alley—the third Theatre Royal after London's Covent Garden and Drury Lane—saw Shakespeare on its boards from its early days. One of the first productions at the theatre was *Othello*, staged in November 1662, in the month after opening its doors. There are eleven extant 1670s prompt-books for Shakespeare plays at the theatre and evidence that at least two more once existed. The prompt-books comprise some of our earliest evidence for how Shakespeare was performed during this period—both in Ireland and elsewhere—and confirm that Shakespeare was a vital component of the nascent theatre's repertoire. Smock Alley's commitment to Shakespeare extended across the Restoration period and well into the eighteenth century.

This tradition was entrenched under the management of Thomas Sheridan—godson of Jonathan Swift and father to the dramatist Richard Brinsley Sheridan—in the 1740s and

'ALL THE WORLD'S A STAGE'—THEOBALD WOLFE TONE AND SHAKESPEARE

Above: The only surviving illustration of Dublin's Smock Alley theatre. Built in 1662, it was the third Theatre Royal after London's Covent Garden and Drury Lane, and saw Shakespeare on its boards from its early days. (*Gentleman's Magazine*, London, June 1789)

'50s. Sheridan's project was to increase Shakespeare's reputation amongst the Dublin audience with his regular and wildly popular 'Shakespeare Series'. These were subscription-based programmes of Shakespeare plays, taking place as many as three times a year, which saw between six and eight plays performed at a rate of one or two a week. During Sheridan's tenure at Smock Alley he staged eighteen of Shakespeare's plays in over 295 performances.

PRINT
By Tone's time, moreover, Shakespeare was a well-established presence not only in Dublin's theatres but also in its bookshops. The ever-growing popularity of Shakespeare on the stage was actively supported by a thriving print industry, which churned out copies of the plays throughout the first half of the eighteenth century. Andrew Murphy calculates that between 1725 and 1800 up to 50 separate Irish publishers produced almost 80 different editions of Shakespeare—both of individual plays and of the complete works. Shakespeare plays produced at Smock Alley were often coupled with a new print edition of the play, evidence that the plays on stage were appreciated in private too. Sheridan's devotion to Shakespeare, complemented by the steady stream of cheap editions of the plays and poems, was part of a widespread and steady deification of the dramatist in eighteenth-century culture—the vanguard of this movement being led, most famously, by David Garrick in London. Shakespeare was in the air. Though Dublin has received less attention in histories of Shakespeare performance, Augustan Dublin rivalled London in its frenzy for the playwright.

TONE'S 'ESSENTIALLY LITERARY' IMAGINATION
Thomas Bartlett avers that an 'essential fact concerning Tone' is that 'he was from first to last an eighteenth-century figure'. Crucially, the figure of Shakespeare that is so recognisable to us is also a product of the eighteenth century. This was the century in which, as Jonathan Bate writes, Shakespeare 'rose through the ranks of poets and assumed his status as supreme "genius"'. In this context, then, it is not surprising that Tone was familiar with the works of Shakespeare. However, the combination of Tone's particular penchant for the theatre and what Jim Smyth has described as his 'essentially literary' imagination left behind a clear and recoverable veneration for the dramatist that outstrips his admiration for any other author, literary or political. Tone credited Shakespeare with an intimate knowledge of human nature, and he turns to Shakespeare to express sentiments about love, honour, war and death. In his surviving writing—diaries, correspondence and political publications—Tone quotes from at least 24 of Shakespeare's plays, totalling almost 125 citations.

It is important to note, however, that Tone's habit of quoting Shakespeare—though it gives us

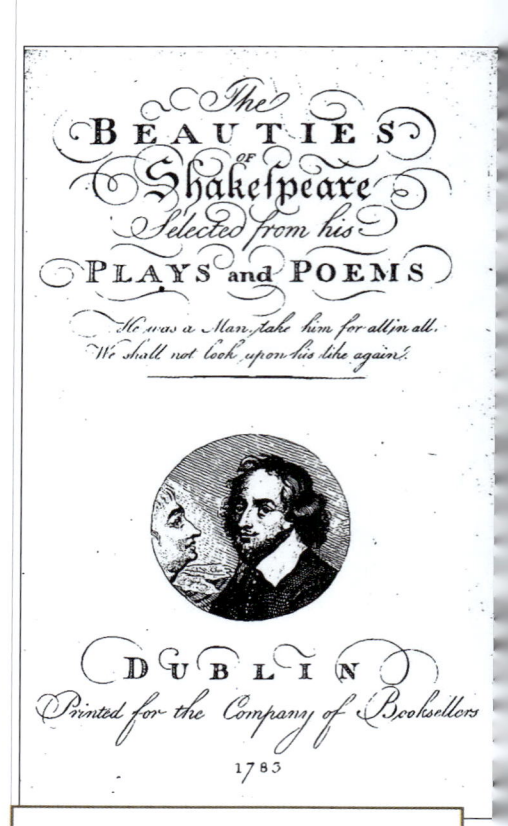

Above: Title-page of a Dublin edition of William Dodd's *The beauties of Shakespeare*, the first anthology of Shakespeare-specific quotations, published in 1783, two years after Tone entered Trinity College. (Eighteenth-Century Collections Online)

important insight into his sense of humour, his classical ideals and his

> '... the actor in Tone was instinctive. It explains the ease with which he could cast aside practicalities and assume the role of romantic hero.'

romantic notions about war—was not unusual in his time. For the eighteenth-century intellectual, a working knowledge of Shakespeare, and a peacocking ability to quote him, was a kind of shorthand for sophistication. References to Shakespeare played an important role in the dramatist's rising reputation. Fiona Ritchie and R.S. White suggest that during this period Shakespeare 'was constructed through frequent quotation as object of uncritical admiration, touchstone of literary or theatrical quality, font of wisdom, cultural capital and moral authority'. The publication of William Dodd's *The beauties of Shakespeare* (1752)—the first anthology of Shakespeare-specific quotations—underscores the cultural currency associated with Shakespearean citation. The collection's immense popularity and frequent reprints are a strong indication of the contemporary vogue for quoting Shakespeare; a Dublin edition of the anthology appeared two years after Tone entered Trinity College. Such an edition made it possible for anyone to procure a Shakespeare quote regardless of whether or not they had seen the play in performance or read the text.

TONE 'SOMEWHAT OF AN ACTOR'

It is in Tone's student years—and in his year away from the College—that we find the first indications of the depth of his interest in theatre. During his exile from Trinity in 1783 Tone himself dabbled in acting, though it seems that he had acted in amateur productions before 1783, describing himself as already 'somewhat of an actor' in his recollection of that year. We know with certainty that he appeared in two productions at the newly constructed Kirwan's Lane theatre in Galway—acting opposite Eliza Martin, with whom he fell in love during his extended visits to the Martins between 1783 and 1785, and who shared his passion for amateur theatricals.

The relationship between Martin and Tone never developed into a full-blown affair, but Tone reflects that by acting out 'particular situations with her, both in rehearsals and on the stage', he 'very soon became in love to a degree almost inconceivable'. The love affair was, as Marianne Elliot writes, 'an extension of the unreal world of the theatre in which it had first developed'. Importantly, Elliot observes that 'the actor in Tone was instinctive. It explains the ease with which he could cast aside practicalities and assume the role of romantic hero.' This theatrical romanticism was rooted not just in his own forays onto the stage but also in his regular visits to the theatre.

Though we do not have anything close to a comprehensive record of Tone's theatre attendance, it is evident enough that theatre-going was a regular part of his life: as a young man in Dublin, as a law student in London, on political business in Belfast, and as a republican emissary in Paris where, in 1796, he waited on the outcomes of his negotiations and had 'nothing to write of but the theatres of the boulevards!'. For Tone, the 'French comedians are infinitely beyond the English', and it is in Tone's commentary on the theatres in Paris that we find tangible evidence of his close familiarity with the theatres in London. 'The Drury Lane of Paris', he labels the Théâtre de la rue Feydeau. 'Set the ballets of [London's] Haymarket beside this!', he writes in a favourable review of *L'offrande à la liberté* at the Grande Opéra, Théâtre des Arts. But where French ballets and comedians won Tone's approval, their renditions of Shakespeare did not impress him: 'Went to see *Othello*, not translated but only "taken from the English". Poor Shakespeare! I felt for him. The French tragedy is a pitiful performance.' After a French *Macbeth* that he saw the following month, he writes of the actress in the role of Lady Macbeth that she was 'very good, if I had not seen Mrs Siddons, before whom all the actresses here vanish'.

Tone would certainly have attended the theatre in June 1784, when the celebrated Sarah Siddons appeared in Dublin for the season. In fact, Siddons appeared in the same play in which Tone had acted at Galway in the preceding year: John Home's *Douglas*. With Siddons taking up Eliza Martin's role as Lady Randolph, Tone would surely have been drawn to the theatre that

Above: A 1761 Dublin edition of *Macbeth* 'as performed at the Theatres in *London* and *Dublin*'. (Eighteenth-Century Collections Online)

'ALL THE WORLD'S A STAGE'—THEOBALD WOLFE TONE AND SHAKESPEARE

Above: Mrs Sarah Siddons, the most celebrated actress of the eighteenth century, by Thomas Gainsborough (1785). In 1784 she appeared in Dublin in the same play in which Tone had acted at Galway in the preceding year—John Home's *Douglas*.

summer. Siddons, however, was most famed for her roles in Shakespeare's plays, and it was for her association with the dramatist that Tone and his fellows in the College Historical Society proposed to recognise the actress. The society raised a motion to present her with a copy of the Oxford edition of Shakespeare's complete works. This was not enough for some, however, who suggested that the actress instead be presented with a gold medal—such was the regard of Tone and his contemporaries for interpretation of Shakespeare.

SEAMLESSLY INTERLACED CITATIONS
Tone himself offers some level of interpretation in his litany of Shakespeare quotations: he doesn't always quote correctly, and sometimes he changes words to suit his purpose. The citations are interlaced with his own words—often seamlessly, sometimes slightly impenetrably ('I do not see what the deuce that applys [*sic*] to, but no matter', he writes after a *Richard III* reference), and almost always without naming the author—in a way that feels unfamiliar to us. Shakespeare was always on the tip of his tongue. It seems that this was a characteristic that bled into his life off the page and dated back as far as his days at Revd Craig's school on Henry Street.

George Miller, his schoolmate and contemporary at Trinity, recalled that Tone 'had a great facility in quoting Shakespeare, and raising a laugh by a pun'. The caricature of Tone in *Belmont Castle*, the satirical novel that he wrote with friends while at the Middle Temple, has a partiality for speaking in quotations and in verse. Indeed, Tone seems to have quoted Shakespeare, among other writers, not only to show off his wit but also as a bit of good fun. In a letter to Matilda written in March 1797, he remarks that in a previous letter 'there were divers quotations well worth their weight in gold [which] I laughed myself excessively at writing, as I have no doubt you did at reading them'. He signs off with a quote from *The Merry Wives of Windsor*. In a letter of May 1798, Tone quotes from Shakespeare and Swift, and concludes that 'this is a vile and unconnected letter, but it is written *after dinner*, as the style and penmanship will witness' and 'is made up of nothing but quotations!'. We might glean from these instances a sense of both the fun that Tone had with Shakespeare and the way in which Shakespeare's language was a spirited part of Tone's rhetoric, even when inebriated.

As these letters suggest, Shakespeare served as a touchstone in Tone's epistolary relationship with Matilda, and as a way through which he expressed his love for her. This would have pleased Matilda, for whom Shakespeare was 'the sublime Bard'. 'Live unbruised, and love our babies', Tone writes in the summer of 1797, borrowing from *Much Ado About Nothing*. In a letter of August 1798 he emphasises his devotion, signing off as Hamlet writing to Ophelia: 'Thine, while this machine is to him!'. In a letter the following month, from 'L'Adujant-Genéral T. Wolfe Tone' and under the heading 'Erin Go Bragh, Liberté, Égalité', Matilda is addressed as Brutus's Portia: 'you are my true and honourable wife'. That, Tone writes, 'is saying enough'. Shakespeare's Portia is 'a woman well-reputed [and] Cato's daughter'. This is the same Cato of Joseph Addison's eighteenth-century play, whose suicide was a symbol of classical republican gesture. Portia, too, typifies the strong Roman woman; she wounds her own thigh, in an act of blood-letting associated with classical values, to prove to Brutus that he should confide in her. Thus for Tone, in his final year and in the face of the failure of the republic, all his sentiment for his wife is bound up in the classical ideal of the honourable wife.

HENRY V

Shakespeare also provides Tone with a language of war and romantic heroism throughout 1796. In February, both *Macbeth* and *Richard II* furnish him with a vocabulary of bravery; 'hang those that talk of fear!', he writes of their military plans, for 'ten thousand hearts are great within [his] bosom'. In August he articulates his zeal and his impatience with words from *Richard III* (Colley Cibber's stage version): 'my soul's in arms, and eager for the fray'. As he anxiously awaits the departure of the French fleet for Ireland, he quotes—rather ironically—from the battle of Agincourt and the prologue to *Henry V*, writing that 'everything now seems to "give dreadful note of preparation"'. Aboard ship, facing an interminable fog, Tone again draws on *Henry V* in making his case that the ships should try to land. 'If we are doomed to die,' he writes, 'we are enough | To do our country loss, and if to live | The fewer men, the greater share of honour.' In these moments Shakespeare's words articulate for Tone his conviction that this was an honourable pursuit—that should they die in the name of the republic that would be enough. *Henry V* loomed large in Tone's mind during the aborted attempt on Ireland; he describes the ragtag group of French soldiers with another (slight mis-) quotation, 'There's not a rag of feather in our army | Good argument, I hope, we will not fly', and goes on to highlight how much the play has dominated his thoughts—'It is inconceivable how well that most inconceivable of all writers, Shakespeare, has hit off the French character, in his play of Henry 5th. I have been struck with it fifty times this evening.' It is not too far-fetched to conclude that Tone had a copy of *Henry V* on board with him, and that he whiled away the hours waiting for a break in the weather with this text, traditionally associated with English military might but here repurposed in service of the Irish cause.

Shakespeare also provides a language through which Tone articulates or muses on death in the context of revolution. Hamlet's reflections on death—and, indeed, suicide—are familiar to Tone. 'In times of revolution', he writes, 'it is a short journey sometimes from the prison to that undiscovered country from whose bourne no traveller returns.' In June 1796 Tone records that, in conversation with a French officer, he made 'many fine observations, stolen from Shakespeare, on the folly of fearing death in public situations'. That Shakespeare offered him this framework is demonstrated by Tone's reaction to the execution of a fellow United Irishman, James Quigley, on 7 June 1798. Quigley acted as an agent for the United Irishmen in Britain and made several journeys to

Above: Elisabetta Sirani's *Portia wounding her thigh* (1664) typifies the strong Roman woman; the act of blood-letting, associated with classical values, is to prove to her husband, Brutus, that he should confide in her.

France in 1796 and 1797. Arrested at Margate in February 1798, he was sentenced to death on the evidence of seditious papers found in his coat pocket, and by refusing to incriminate others in exchange for his life he sealed his fate. For Tone, Quigley (with whom he had quarrelled) 'died like a hero'. 'If I ever reach Ireland and we establish our liberty', he wrote, 'I will be the first to propose a monument to his memory; his conduct at the hour of his death clears everything:—Nothing in his life | Became him like the leaving of it.' These words, from Shakespeare's *Macbeth*, give us a visceral insight into Tone's philosophy of the honourable death, and into what guided his hand in November 1798.

● *Eilís Smyth is an Irish Research Council-funded post-doctoral fellow at Trinity College, Dublin.*

FURTHER READING

J. Maxwell & K. Rumbold (eds), *Shakespeare and quotation* (Cambridge, 2018).

C. Morash, *A history of Irish theatre 1601–2000* (Cambridge, 2002).

A. Murphy, *Shakespeare in print* (Cambridge, 2021).

MATILDA TONE—'A WORTHY RELICT'

BY **CATRIONA KENNEDY**

Above: Mrs Sarah Siddons in the role of Matilda, Lady Randolph, in John Home's popular 1756 historical tragedy *Douglas*. In identifying and renaming his wife as this tragic character, was Tone furnishing a script for her role as wife and then widow? (V&A Museums)

IN THE EARLY 1950s, Rosamond Jacob, a Quaker, feminist and republican, author of several novels and a well-received history of the United Irishmen, was working on a biography of Theobald Wolfe Tone's widow, Matilda Tone (1769–1849). Having struggled to find a publisher for the biography, she shifted course and began writing a historical novel based on Matilda's life that was eventually published in 1957. Jacob's efforts to reconstruct the life and worlds of Matilda Tone in history and then in fiction speak to the status that Tone's widow had achieved within republican memory. By the twentieth century she was tightly woven into the weft of her husband's romantic narrative, familiar to readers of Tone's autobiography as the steadfast wife who had uncomplainingly supported her husband's republican ambitions. Jacob's project seems to have been motivated by a desire to draw out Matilda Tone from under the shadow of her husband. In the manuscript of the original biography she speculated that Matilda likely supported Tone's vision of an Ireland 'where brotherhood came before dogma' not 'because "my husband thinks", but because she thought herself'. Nevertheless, the changing titles for this work and the shift from historical biography to historical fiction underline just how challenging this endeavour was. The original title of Jacob's biography, 'Matilda Tone', signalled an attempt to approach her as a figure in her own right; the title of the final published version, *The rebel's wife*, saw Matilda once more subsumed into the identity of her famous husband.

Tone's admiration for his wife is a recurring theme in his journals. They were partly addressed to her and repeatedly praised her courage, unstinting support for his ambitions and cheerfulness in adversity.

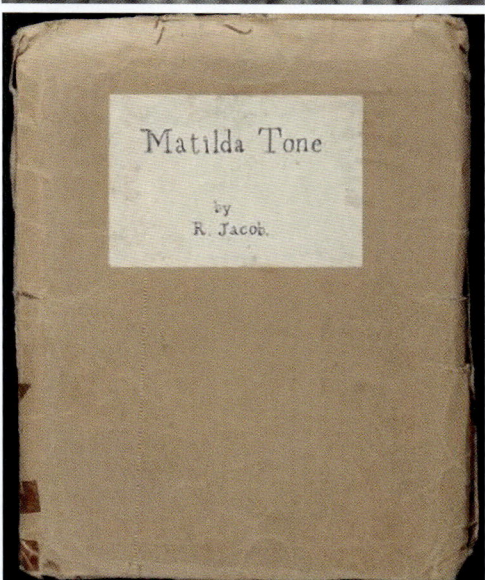

Above: Rosamond Jacob and the title-page of her manuscript biography of Matilda Tone. (Rosamond Jacob Papers, NLI)

Remembered as an intelligent and astute woman by those who knew her, Matilda Tone nonetheless remains a shadowy figure. There is, for example, no known portrait of her and, while her surviving letters suggest a skilled writer and perceptive political commentator, her archive is scattered and fragmentary. Only 29 years old when Wolfe Tone died, Matilda would live for another 50 years in exile in Paris and later the United States, during which time she became an exemplary 'republican relict': a relict in both the arcane sense, meaning a widow, but also a venerated object associated with the deceased. Cast in the role of mourner-in-chief for her husband and guardian of his memory, Matilda Tone both conformed to and sometimes resisted the various scripts that were written for her.

FROM MARTHA TO MATILDA

The name by which she would be known, Matilda, was not the name with which she was christened. Born Martha Witherington to a reasonably prosperous Dublin merchant family, she was only fifteen when she first met Tone, through her brother, a fellow student at Trinity College, Dublin, and barely sixteen when she married him against her parents' wishes in 1785. It was Tone who bestowed upon her the name Matilda in reference to the character of Matilda, Lady Randolph, in the Scottish dramatist John Home's popular 1756 historical tragedy *Douglas*. This was a role closely associated with the most celebrated actress of the eighteenth century, Sarah Siddons, but it was also a part associated with Tone's youthful infatuation with a married woman, Elizabeth Martin, who had played Lady Randolph opposite Tone in a production of *Douglas* in Galway in 1783. As later biographers of Tone would note, this renaming of his future wife after a part played by a former *amour* seems insensitive, though not out of character given Tone's immersion in the world of theatre and propensity for theatrical gestures. More significantly, perhaps, in identifying Matilda with this tragic character he was furnishing a script for her role as wife and then widow: in Home's play, Matilda remains faithful to the memory of her first husband after his death in battle, providing a powerful portrait of uxorial fidelity in tragic circumstances.

As Nancy Curtin has explored in her study of Matilda Tone, the classical republican tradition, a significant influence on the United Irishmen, would also offer a script for the performance of these roles. Looking to classical antiquity for inspiration, this political tradition elaborated a model of republican femininity derived from the virtuous matrons of ancient Rome and figures such as Portia, wife of Brutus, who had supported her husband's efforts to save the Roman republic from tyranny. It provided an austere but culturally significant model for the political partnership between husband and wife, according to which women were best able to serve the cause of the republic by ruthlessly suppressing their personal feelings and interests, and willingly sacrificing their husbands and sons to the public good. It is possible to trace Matilda's fulfilment of this republican ideal in her willingness to allow her husband to pursue his political ambitions despite the great cost to her and her family. She followed him into exile in the United States in 1795 and, in the ultimate act of republican sacrifice, would not reveal to Tone that she was pregnant when, six months later, he left once again for France. As Tone recorded in his memoir, the night before they parted: 'the courage and firmness of the women supported me … we had neither tears

> **'It was Tone who bestowed upon her the name Matilda in reference to the character of Matilda, Lady Randolph, in the Scottish dramatist John Home's popular 1756 historical tragedy *Douglas*.'**

nor lamentations, but, on the contrary, the most ardent hope and the most steady resolution'.

A WIDOW IN PARIS

In 1797 Matilda crossed the Atlantic once again to join Tone in Paris, and it was in Paris that she would learn the news of Tone's death in November 1798. The circumstances in which Matilda found herself after Tone's death were undeniably desperate. She was grief-stricken and

HISTORY IRELAND/ **57**

MATILDA TONE—'A WORTHY RELICT'

Above: Lucien Bonaparte, president of the ruling Council of Five Hundred in 1798, was so impressed by an interview with Matilda that he not only paid tribute to Wolfe Tone as 'an illustrious martyr of liberty' but also praised her 'independent spirit and firmness'.

alone with three young children in what would turn out to be permanent exile from Ireland and, according to her son William, had only limited French. Despite this, she would prove remarkably resourceful in ensuring that she and her family were provided for, arranging a personal interview with Lucien Bonaparte, the president of the ruling Council of Five Hundred, in which she pressed her case for a more generous pension for her and her family in recognition of Tone's services as a fallen French officer. Bonaparte was so moved by her intervention that, in a speech supporting additional provision for Matilda and her children, he not only paid tribute to Wolfe Tone as 'an illustrious martyr of liberty' but also invoked the spirit of classical antiquity in his praise of Matilda's 'independent spirit and firmness'. He compared her to the women of ancient Sparta, who, when their countrymen returned from battle, would anxiously scan the returning ranks and, on finding their husbands, brothers or sons absent, exclaim: 'He died for his country; he died for the republic'.

According to the demands made of Matilda as a republican widow, having sacrificed her husband to the nation she was now expected to dedicate her life to preserving Tone's heroic memory and raising her children in his image. Her performance of this role was further encouraged by her continued contact with United Irish exiles in Paris and the United States, who were able to commemorate Tone openly in a manner that was then impossible in Ireland. On a visit to New York from Paris in 1807, she accepted a pendant from the Hibernian Provident Society of New York, inscribed to the 'worthy relict of the late Illustrious

Right: The pendant, inscribed to the 'worthy relict of the late Illustrious Patriot Gen. Theobald Wolfe Tone', presented to Matilda by the Hibernian Provident Society on her visit to New York from Paris in 1807. (Fonsie Mealy)

Patriot Gen. Theobald Wolfe Tone'. In a further allusion to classical Rome and to Tone's death, the obverse depicted the suicide of Cato the Younger, his final gesture of defiance against Julius Caesar's tyranny. On the same occasion, the Society presented her sixteen-year-old son, William, with a sword, expressing their hope that it would 'one day in his hands avenge the wrongs of his country'. This was an exacting claim to make on a mother who by 1806 had already lost two of her children to tuberculosis and whose only surviving child, William, was beginning to show signs of the same disease. And it is clear that Matilda resisted some of the demands that were made of her as a republican widow where they conflicted with the interests of her family. In 1802 she tried to dissuade what she described as a 'strange collection of Irishmen in Paris' from recruiting her late husband's younger brother, Arthur Tone, into their schemes for a renewed military expedition to Ireland, pleading with them, in vain, that her children were young and helpless and needed their uncle's protection. While her decision to allow her son to embark on a military career, despite her own misgivings, partly fulfilled Irish republicans' wish to see him follow in his father's footsteps, she came into conflict with Napoleon's minister for war, the Franco-Irish General Henri-Jacques-Guillaume Clarke, when she refused his offer to William to join Napoleon's Irish Legion. Matilda believed that her son's military career would be blighted if he joined this

Right: General Henri-Jacques-Guillaume Clarke—Matilda came into conflict with Napoleon's Franco-Irish minister for war when she refused his offer to her son William to join Napoleon's Irish Legion. (Library of Congress)

HISTORY IRELAND/ 59

MATILDA TONE—'A WORTHY RELICT'

Above: A Charles Codman view of the Kalorama estate, Georgetown, *c.* 1800–25. After their arrival in the United States in 1817, Matilda and her second husband, Thomas Wilson, resided for several years in the west wing.

ragged group of emigrant soldiers. She also bristled at Clarke's condescending proposal that she might join his household as governess and English tutor to his children. 'Not to inhabit the palace of the proudest potentate on earth', she later wrote, 'would I have given up my little home and my freedom, my desolate freedom, to think and to feel.' In one of several instances in Matilda Tone's life where she showed some daring and courage, she accosted Napoleon Bonaparte while he was hunting in the forest of St Germain to beseech him to support her son's naturalisation as a French citizen, so that he could be admitted instead to the prestigious École de Cavalerie.

MRS TONE TO MRS WILSON

In one of Tone's final letters to Matilda, he reminded her that she would have a friend and protector in Thomas Wilson, a Scottish lawyer and reformer whom the Tones had likely first met in the United States and who, it seems, accompanied Matilda on her journey to France to be reunited with her husband in 1797. When Wilson returned to Scotland from Paris in 1802, he continued to correspond with Matilda, and the couple were married in Paris in August 1816. They travelled together to Edinburgh, where they remained until April 1817. When it became clear, however, that Matilda's son, having fought on the side of Napoleon at Waterloo, would not be granted permission to return to Britain or Ireland, the Wilsons determined to join William Tone in the United States. They settled first in Georgetown, where they resided for several years in the west wing of the elegant mansion of Kalorama, home to the American diplomat Joel Barlow and his wife, whom Matilda had befriended in Paris.

Matilda's remarriage does not seem to have compromised her status as Tone's widow and mourner-in-chief. Later nationalists were keen to insist that this was a marriage of friendship, and one tacitly endorsed by Tone himself. By contrast, Pamela Fitzgerald, the widow of Edward Fitzgerald, who shortly after her husband's death had forged an unhappy alliance with the American consul to Hamburg, was viewed more harshly. In the severe judgement of the historian of the United Irishmen Richard Robert Madden, by remarrying she had 'forgot her husband's memory'.

CUSTODIAN OF MEMORY

In the United States Matilda pursued an engaged model of republican widowhood grounded in her status as principal custodian of Tone's memory. In Georgetown she mixed with a well-established community of United Irish émigrés that included the Belfast radical William Sampson, whose daughter, Catherine, William Tone would marry in 1825. In ensuring Tone's enduring reputation amongst Irish nationalists, her most significant contribution would be her collaboration with her son to collate, edit and publish Tone's journals and memoir as the *Life of Theobald Wolfe Tone* in 1826. This drew together the papers that Matilda had carefully preserved through her many painful journeys and displacements. As historians have long noted, without the survival and publication of this moving, evocative record of

Tone's life and career it is doubtful whether he would have achieved

> **'In the United States Matilda pursued an engaged model of republican widowhood grounded in her status as principal custodian of Tone's memory.'**

quite such an exalted position within the pantheon of Irish republican heroes.

The role that Matilda Tone performed in actively guarding and promoting her husband's legacy contrasts with the more passive figure of the grief-stricken woman lamenting her fallen hero that was prevalent in Ireland in the decades following the 1798 rebellion. In a context in which open celebration of the United Irishmen remained legally hazardous, commemoration was necessarily oblique and furtive, more focused on feminine suffering than masculine militarism. This commemorative mode was most fully embodied by the figure of Sarah Curran, fiancée of Robert Emmet, the executed leader of the 1803 United Irish rebellion. Following her doomed love affair with Emmet, Curran had married a British army officer and followed him to Sicily, where she died in 1807 from consumption, though the preferred explanation was that she had pined away from a broken heart. In Thomas Moore's famous elegy on Robert Emmet, 'She is far from the land', Curran was portrayed in mournful exile, 'her heart' in Emmet's grave, singing a plaintive song to the memory of her dead lover. In this sentimental depiction Curran was cast as an eternal mourner—an emblem of the feminised nation grieving her fallen martyrs.

Matilda Tone, by contrast, seems to have resisted efforts to cast her as the eternal mourner in the mode of Sarah Curran. Indeed, her decision to publish Tone's *Life* in 1826 had been prompted in part by an account of her life in Paris that appeared in the *New Monthly Magazine* in 1825, portraying her as still immured in grief, her home a shrine to her dead husband and children. The anonymous author suggested that Matilda had been reluctant to remarry, thinking it due to 'the memory of her husband that she should bear no other name'. Describing a visit to Matilda on the eve of her wedding in 1816, he wrote:

'She happened to be alone, was unusually sad, and for the first time that I had seen her, dressed in white … my eye passed involuntarily to the portrait of Tone, which hung immediately before her. She rose and retired, in silence and in tears.'

In a statement appended to the 1826 edition of Tone's *Life*, Matilda rejected this mawkish vignette, dismissing it as a 'hackneyed and commonplace novel scene'. Protesting at this attempt to recast the details of her life as a sentimental fiction, she insisted that she did not own a white dress, had never noticed where the gentleman's eyes had glanced

Below: William Sampson—in Georgetown, Matilda mixed with a well-established community of United Irish émigrés that included the Belfast radical Sampson, whose daughter, Catherine, William Tone would marry in 1825. (Madden, *United Irishmen*/NLI).

and had certainly not left the room in tears.

THE 'HEARTBROKEN' WIDOW
While Matilda bridled at such depictions, she would continue to assert her status as principal guardian of Tone's memory until the end of her life. When Richard Robert Madden published the first edition of his monumental collective biography of the United Irishmen in 1842, she wrote to the *New York Truth-Teller* newspaper to correct publicly what she believed were inaccuracies in Madden's account of Tone's role in the movement, and to challenge Madden's contention that it was Tone who had been responsible for steering the United Irishmen in a more revolutionary direction. She was particularly aggrieved that Madden had not made the effort to visit her during his two research trips amongst the United Irish exiles in the United States. In this she proved herself ready, when provoked, to present herself as the 'heartbroken' widow, writing that 'perhaps he [Madden] was ignorant of my existence, for I live in complete retirement, and to use Carolan's words—"Lonely and desolate I mourn the dead"'.

The image of mournful retirement that Matilda Tone presented in her letter to the *New York Truth-Teller* belies, however, her continued engagement with radical and revolutionary politics. We know from her correspondence with Eliza Fletcher, like Matilda a veteran of 1790s radicalism and widow of a Scottish reformer, that she retained a keen interest in contemporary affairs. The two women enthusiastically followed and applauded the progress of the wars of liberation in Latin America, the Greek war of independence and, in February 1848, a year before Matilda's death, revolution once again in Paris. 'Vive la République!!', Fletcher wrote excitedly to Matilda, 'have I not thought of you continually since the 23rd of February? Have you and I slumbered since 1798 only to be awaken'd once more by the *tocsin* sounding in the streets of Paris?'

AN ILLUSTRIOUS IRISHWOMAN
That same year would also see a short-lived rising in Ireland, led by the Young Ireland movement, who from the 1840s had championed the 'cult of Tone'. Central to that cult was the identification and preservation of Tone's grave at Bodenstown, Co. Kildare. In this, too, Matilda Tone played a key role. It was at her behest that Thomas Davis erected a marble slab at the site of Tone's grave. Although Davis never completed his planned biography of Tone, he drafted a dedication to Matilda, in which he paid tribute to this 'worthy relict', judging her 'the only fit guardian of this memoir of him who lies in Bodenstown'. The Young Ireland writers would also be responsible for elevating Matilda from an adjunct in the construction of her husband's heroic identity to an exemplary figure in her own right. In April 1848,

> '... his widow was presented to Irish women as encapsulating the more passive heroism that the nation demanded of them.'

only a few months before the Young Ireland rising, the *Nation* newspaper began a series entitled 'Illustrious Irishwomen', the stated aim of which was to 'place before our countrywomen a mirror, in which they will see their duties in the struggle for which Ireland is now preparing'. The series opened, significantly, with a biography of Matilda Tone published in instalments over several weeks. Just as Tone had become the heroic embodiment of the spirit of the Irish nation, now his widow was presented to Irish women as encapsulating the more passive heroism that the nation demanded of them. This entailed fortitude, self-sacrifice and unwavering support for their menfolk.

In many ways, nationalist hagiographies of Matilda Tone and other republican widows provided a frustratingly limited template for Irish women's political action in the late nineteenth and twentieth centuries, insofar as they presented women's ideological commitments as mediated entirely through their male relatives and as best expressed through sacrifice and dutiful remembrance. In Helena Concannon's nationalist history *The women of 'Ninety-Eight* (1919), published on the eve of the War of Independence and dedicated to the women, both living and dead, 'who had given their dear ones to Ireland', Matilda Tone's biography was gathered together with the other 'Wives of 'Ninety-Eight'. In this way, this intriguing, intelligent and courageous woman continued to be overshadowed by her husband. It is in part because Matilda fulfilled the role of republican relict so well that it remains difficult to see her as a figure in her own right and to ask, as Rosamond Jacob asked, what she herself thought—to see her as more than the 'rebel's wife'.

- *Catriona Kennedy is Senior Lecturer in Modern History at the University of York.*

FURTHER READING
D. Brundage, 'Matilda Tone in America: exile, gender, and memory in the making of Irish republican nationalism', *New Hibernia Review* 14 (1) (2010), 96–111.

N. Curtin, 'Matilda Tone and virtuous republican femininity', in D. Keogh & N. Furlong (eds), *The women of 1798* (Dublin, 1998).

C. Kennedy, 'Republican relics: gender, memory, and mourning in Irish nationalist culture, c. 1798–1848', *Journal of British Studies* 59 (3) (2020), 608–37.

R.R. Madden, *The United Irishmen, their lives and times* (7 vols) (1842–60).

J. Rendall, '"Friends of liberty & virtue": women radicals and transatlantic correspondence, 1789–1848', in M. Cross & C. Bland (eds), *Gender and politics in the age of letter writing, 1750–2000* (Aldershot, 2004).

A MEETING WITH MATILDA—
THOMAS CATHER'S *VOYAGE TO AMERICA*

BY **WILLA MURPHY**

IN 1836 A YOUNG Ulsterman made a pilgrimage to Georgetown, near Washington DC, to meet the formidable widow of Theobald Wolfe Tone. In his journal he records that 'she is a very fine old lady, with wonderful vivacity, and still retains a strong touch of the brogue on the tongue and heart—her feelings are enthusiastically Irish'.

OLD WORLD DISAPPROVAL
Thomas Cather, son of landed gentry from Limavady, Co. Derry, was just 23 when he set sail for the New World with his friend Henry Tyler. Suffering from a touch of *ennui*, the wealthy schoolfriends sought relief in a hazardous Atlantic crossing and a year-long adventure in a rough-around-the-edges young country. Cather's Grand Tour took him from New York to New Orleans, down corduroy roads, up the Mississippi, across the frontier and into Indian country. He discussed politics with Andrew Jackson and lived for a month among the Pottawatomi Indians. In Philadelphia he viewed the Jeffersonian manuscript of the Declaration of Independence, and he was among the first visitors to the newly built tourist infrastructure at Niagara Falls. His journal, *Voyage to America*, forms part of the long tradition of European travel writing about the Americas and includes familiar Old World disapproval of American coarseness and greed. Everywhere he goes, Cather finds Americans moving fast, talking fast and eating faster. 'The first morning at breakfast I was absolutely astounded at the rapidity of their jaws', he writes on 8 March 1836. And, not unlike Wolfe Tone, he is disappointed to find the sons of the Republic venerating the purse above all else—'the eternal song is about dollars, dollars, dollars!' Cather's journal is a sharp account of American habits and culture, but it also offers a fascinating snapshot of the aging exiles of 1798. For a young man who grew up with the stories and spectres of '98 in Ulster, America is mediated in part through a United Irish prism.

THE CATHERS OF LIMAVADY AND THE SAMPSONS
The Cathers of Limavady were significant developers of the town in the nineteenth century. Landowners and successful businessmen, they owned farms, mills, distilleries and breweries, and provided Limavady with its bankers, sheriffs and magistrates. They built the Second

Below: Limavady's Second Presbyterian Church, built by the Cathers in 1840.

Bottom: The Cather distillery on the edge of the town. They were also involved in the Temperance Hall at its centre.

HISTORY IRELAND/ **63**

A MEETING WITH MATILDA—THOMAS CATHER'S *VOYAGE TO AMERICA*

Presbyterian Church and converted the local courthouse into a brewery. The Cather women were heavily involved in the Temperance movement. Thus the canny family ran both the distillery on the edge of town and the Temperance Hall in its centre.

It was the family's connections with the Sampsons, however, that gave Cather's journey to America its United Irish inflection. George Vaughan Sampson was the beloved rector of Limavady's Aghanloo Parish. A progressive social reformer and author of the magisterial *Statistical survey of the County Londonderry* (1802), George moved in the same social circles as the Cathers. It is likely that as a boy Thomas attended George's funeral in 1827, one of the largest ever seen in the county. It was through the Sampson family that Cather arrived in New York with a letter of introduction to George's youngest brother, the exiled United Irishman William Sampson (whose daughter was married to Wolfe Tone's son). As an attorney, Sampson made his name during a famous case in 1813, when he successfully defended the secrecy of the confessional and the right of the priest not to testify against his parishioners (arguably channelling Tone's impassioned defence of the rights of Irish Catholics).

'IRISH FEELING'

Thomas Cather's first week in America was punctuated by visits to the Sampson home, where he met another exiled United Irishman, Dr William James MacNevin. On 10 March 1836 the journal records:

'Spent a pleasant evening at Mr Sampson's—met there Dr. MacNevin, a fine animated, intelligent old gentleman, with a great deal of good, Irish feeling. Next morning he paid us a visit, which we returned, and had the pleasure of being introduced to Mrs M, and the young ladies—engaged to spend the next evening there [...]

Monday evening we spent at Dr. MacNevin's. The more I know the more I like him and Mr. Sampson, who, with his daughter, Mrs Tone, was there to meet us. I had a great "palaver" with the two old gentlemen on Irish history and antiquities, and heard many stories of the men of '98. The two Misses MacN., pleasing, ladylike girls … We had music and singing, and spent a delightful evening.'

The language of feeling is worth noting here. Again and again, Cather describes the 'Irish feeling' of the men and women of '98. Matilda Tone has 'feelings that are enthusiastically Irish'; Sampson and MacNevin have 'a great deal of good, Irish feeling'. In such passages, Cather's journal evokes the intersection of affection and politics, of emotion and revolution, so characteristic of the United Irish movement. (And a few years later, Fenian sympathiser Walt Whitman would harness such energies in poetry that would make brotherly affection a signpost of American democracy.)

TWO OPPOSING ENERGIES?

Cather's sometimes sentimental journey includes visits to Irish- (and particularly Ulster-) Americans in New York, Philadelphia, Washington

Below: William James MacNevin, the last surviving United Irish leader in exile—'a fine animated, intelligent old gentleman, with a great deal of good, Irish feeling', according to Cather's journal. (Madden, *United Irishmen*/NLI)

WILLIAM JAMES MACNEVEN M.D.

and the Shenandoah Valley. It is a reminder of the massive migration from Ulster to America, migrants described by Patrick Griffin as 'a people perfectly suited to the world of motion they inhabited and came to define'. Cather's sketch of Andrew Jackson, another son of Ulster, is emblematic of this kinetic energy: 'His whole life has been a constant scene of violence and excitement', writes Cather, describing him as full of 'uncontrollable energy' and 'bursts of passion'. Here and elsewhere Cather distinguishes between feeling and passion, between emotion and commotion. On the frontier and along the banks of the Mississippi he finds 'wild untamed men' of 'savage independence' who, like their president, have 'a touch of the earthquake' about them. The Jacksonian American is 'amenable to no law, he wanders where he pleases, he is not troubled with neighbours; he does not want to be *crowded*, as he says'. In Cather's vision we find two opposing (Ulster?) energies at work in America—republican values of liberty and fraternity, and a Jacksonian individualism, an 'unaccommodating take-care-of-myself spirit [obliging] everyone to be as rude and rough as [their] neighbours'.

It is perhaps worth noting that Cather also registers in his journal the death of another violent son of Ulster, Davy Crockett. As he moves through America, Cather's observations might be understood as informed by the late nights with Sampson and MacNevin that began his journey. Their stories and songs of the men of '98 offer lenses through which to view the vast new country, and values against which to measure it. He meditates on the fact that in America 'there are no classic spots' like cathedrals, castles or ruins, 'but', he decides, 'there are places on which Americans may look with just pride. They may point with triumph to the site of those battlefields where undisciplined peasants fought the good fight of liberty and elevated their country from the degraded state of a province to the dignity of an independent nation.'

ANTI-SLAVERY

Cather sounds like Paine or Tone when he lashes out against slavery and the treatment of the Indians: 'this is the strange language and inconsistent conduct on the part of men who boast of their country as being peculiarly the Land of Liberty, and who refer with pride to their Declaration of Independence, in which it is asserted that all mankind are born equal. With what face can they talk of the equality of human rights, they who are traffickers in human flesh?' His expedition into Pottawatomi country in northern Indiana convinces him that they are his 'red brothers', much more so than the 'wild untamed men' of the frontier. (It is worth mentioning that his sojourn with his 'red brothers' happened somewhere near the current location of the University of Notre Dame, home of the 'Fighting Irish'.) And, in an extraordinary passage, Cather offers a counterfactual history that surely finds inspiration in the French landing in Mayo and the United Irish march to Dublin:

'If America had gone to war with France, and the latter power had landed a force in Florida or Louisiana, and then armed the slaves and called to their assistance the Indians ... what would have been the result? What chance would the white population of the Southern States, scattered thinly over a great extent of country, have had against at the same time, a foreign enemy, their own slaves in revolt, and an active and relentless Indian foe?'

Cather foresees a future threat to the American republic whereby 'a popular chief like General Jackson could turn Congress out of doors and establish a military despotism'. He is not hopeful about a country steeped in violence, racism and savage individualism. Towards the end of his journal, he suggests that American national character is the logical extension of the worst of British identity:

'The character of the American nation is fundamentally that of the British ... while they have many of the virtues of the English, they have also their vices pushed to excess, and besides several more of their own growth. They possess great intelligence, energy, enterprise, and perseverance, all the elements necessary to make a flourishing commercial people, but they lack the qualities of a noble and generous nation. Their courage degenerates into ferocity, their love of liberty into licentiousness, and their commercial enterprise into a sordid and mercenary spirit.'

Thomas Cather spent one of his last nights in America with a 'miserably ill' William Sampson, 'death ... written on his brow'. Within a month Sampson was dead, as Cather sailed back to Derry over the 'indescribably uproarious' Atlantic.

● *Willa Murphy lectures in English at Ulster University.*

FURTHER READING

R. Boyd, *The Cambridge Companion to Democracy in America* (Cambridge, 2022).
T. Cather, *Voyage to America* (New York, 1961).
R.R. Madden, *The United Irishmen, their lives and times* (7 vols) (1842–60).

THEOBALD WOLFE TONE FITZGERALD— 1798 IN 1916

BY **DONAL FALLON**

TWO EVENTS THAT captivated nationalist Ireland at the very end of the nineteenth century could not have been more different. Kevin O'Sheil, later a high court judge, recalled how 'in the last years of the last century the Boer War dominated every other topic. Outside town and country politics, the Boer War provided the only other excitement that then stirred citizens in any degree.' The conflict, which was in fact the Second Boer War, grabbed the attention of the Irish public owing to the

> '... the proposal to send the Boers two Maxim guns named 'Wolfe Tone' and 'Parnell' was loudly cheered.'

active participation of a so-called 'Irish Brigade' on the side of the Boers. At a meeting of over 20,000 people in Beresford Place at the height of the war, the proposal to send the Boers two Maxim guns named 'Wolfe Tone' and 'Parnell' was loudly cheered.

1798 CENTENARY
Yet in 1898, against the backdrop of the centenary of the United Irish rebellion, it was children on whom such names were bestowed. The centenary, in the mind of Seán T. O'Kelly, amounted to nothing less than 'the revival of the national spirit'. Séumas Robinson, a participant in the Easter Rising and later active in the Soloheadbeg ambush which began the War of Independence, recalled the centenary as an introduction to separatism for young people and a break with the thinking of their elders. Their parents had 'become convinced that the British Empire was invincible. They had all the arguments against us young people. Then the '98 centenary celebrations set us youngsters agog and enquiring.'

Reflecting on the commercial dimensions of the centenary, Peter Collins notes that 'Leonard's Chemists in Dublin sold '98 Centenary perfume. Bushmills Whiskey, with its distillery sited in a staunchly Protestant village in County Antrim, proclaimed in advertisements that "True Patriots drank Bushmills". Posters, postcards and novels mostly portrayed the Faith and Fatherland, heroic priest-led peasantry version of '98.'

In the political sphere, the year witnessed a significant political tug of war for the legacy of the United Irish rebellion. While Fenian voices like John O'Leary were initially to the fore of the Provisional Centenary Committee, constitutionalists quickly found themselves seeking to utilise the spirit of the year to heal divisions within the ranks of the post-Parnell Irish Parliamentary Party (IPP). For John Dillon, there was hope that those who had been 'unhappily separated from each other for the past eight years would, in the great centenary celebrations, find a common platform'.

Unsurprisingly, much of the focus of the centenary year in the capital was on Theobald Wolfe Tone. On 15 August, 'Wolfe Tone Day' witnessed the unveiling of a foundation stone for a memorial to Tone at St Stephen's Green (not to be confused with the Edward Delaney memorial to Tone opposite the Shelbourne Hotel; the original monument was intended for the site now occupied by the Royal Dublin Fusiliers' commemorative arch). Reporting on the event, the *Freeman's Journal* noted that 'in extent and in significance the gathering bears comparison with the greatest of all that have gone before it in Irish history'. A different note was struck by *The Standard* in Britain, which commented that 'it may be regrettable that such large numbers of Irishmen should appear to look back wistfully to the unhappy movement which culminated in 1798'.

THEOBALD WOLFE TONE FITZGERALD
Theobald Wolfe Tone Fitzgerald, born on 14 June 1898, was not unique in being endowed with the name of the United Irish leader in the centenary year of his death. There was also Theobald Wolfe Tone Dillon (born 3 October 1898), the son of IPP politician John Dillon. Fitzgerald is a particularly intriguing example of this commemorative practice, however, owing to his significant role in the subsequent revolutionary period. A member of the Na Fianna Éireann boy scout movement, he would paint the 'Irish Republic' flag that flew over the GPO throughout the

Poster for *Wolfe Tone—A Romantic Irish Drama* (1898), a melodrama by J.W. Whitbread (1898). According to Seán T. O'Kelly, the centenary celebrations of 1798 amounted to nothing less than 'the revival of the national spirit'. (NLI)

THEOBALD WOLFE TONE FITZGERALD—1798 IN 1916

Above: Thomas McDonald, Countess Markievicz and Theobald Wolfe Tone Fitzgerald in Waterford in 1917. Local republican Patrick Hearne recalled that Markievicz 'lectured in the City Hall ... She was accompanied by Theo Fitzgerald.' (NLI)

Easter Rising, while going on to oversee the handing over of the viceregal lodge in December 1922 as a captain in the National Army.

The young Fitzgerald attended St Andrew's Christian Brothers' School on Westland Row, a school with a strong nationalist ethos which contributed significantly to the revolutionary movement. In his research, Des Byrne uncovered 36 participants in the Easter Rising and subsequent War of Independence who had graduated from the school, and it says much about the school management that Constance Markievicz was permitted to speak to the students there about Na Fianna Éireann.

Writing on the growth of Na Fianna, Marnie Hay states that, 'during the first seven years of its existence, this nationalist youth organization developed branches in at least nineteen Irish counties—mainly in the cities and larger towns of Leinster, Munster and Ulster—as well as in Glasgow and Liverpool'. Tone was a figure of great importance to the culture of Na Fianna, with a Wolfe Tone *sluaigh* (or branch) named in his honour, while Seán Prendergast recalled that 'our annual pilgrimage to Wolfe Tone's grave at Bodenstown was to us an event of first-rate importance … We always sought to make a gallant show in the march from Sallins to the graveyard. Such pilgrimages were held, and succeeded in keeping the national spirit alive.'

In Dublin, those early members recruited from Westland Row remained particularly close to Countess Markievicz. Seamus Pounch recalled in his statement to the Bureau of Military History (BMH) that 'amongst the leaders a small group used to meet constantly at Surrey House, Leinster Road, the home of the Countess, and there were introduced to every personality of repute who visited the house'. Following a raid in early 1916, the *Workers' Republic* newspaper was anything but discreet about this fact, telling readers: 'No one was in the house except the servants and a few of the boys of the Fianna who make the place their headquarters. While the search was going on these boys and girls kindly entertained the police with songs, music and comforting remarks. Unfortunately, the G Men have no ear for music.'

'IRISH REPUBLIC' FLAG

At Surrey House, Fitzgerald painted the famous flag that would fly over the GPO at Easter 1916. In a joint statement to the BMH, Fitzgerald and Harry Walpole recalled that the 'flag was a Standard made of green poplin. On it was painted Irish Republic in white and orange letters. The flag had a fringe of gold lace. The Flag was made in Fry's Poplin Factory, Cork Street.' Curiously, in a house with which the G Men were clearly familiar, they remembered that 'the flag was on the wall of the top back bedroom for about a week previous to Easter 1916'. There are some contradictions between the account given by Walpole and Fitzgerald and that of Maura O'Neill Mackey in a manuscript held in the National Library of Ireland collections, though she too mentions the role of Fitzgerald in its painting.

Textile conservator Rachel Phelan notes of the flag that 'all 13 letters are freehand and executed with great skill by an experienced hand', recalling that Markievicz had studied fine art. Still, this style of painting was much more synonymous with trades than the arts. The Fitzgerald family

Above: The 'Irish Republic' flag, painted by Theobald Wolfe Tone Fitzgerald, that flew over the GPO at the corner of Prince's Street at Easter 1916. (Rachel Phelan)

were in the business of painting and decorating, with the father, Thomas, listed as 'painting contractor' in the 1911 census, and several children as 'painters'. As Phelan suggests, 'Theo had easy access to a large amount of house paint'.

Later, Walpole recalled the efforts of Fitzgerald to have this flag returned to Ireland:

'Captain Theo Fitzgerald asked Sir Arthur Cope (Under Secretary) to return the flag. Sir Arthur promised he would, but found it was a Regimental Trophy, and could not be interfered with. When this regiment was disbanded this, with other trophies, were presented to the late King George V. I understand it is in the present King's collection. Any officer of the Royal Regiment of the period will remember this flag. It flew upside down in the Regimental Mess.'

BOLAND'S MILLS
For Theobald Wolfe Tone Fitzgerald, Easter Week played out in the vicinity of Boland's Mills. Interned in Richmond Barracks in the aftermath of the insurrection, he returned to Na Fianna Éireann and headquarters staff. When a British Army recruitment streamer appeared festooned across the front of the GPO—a provocative gesture in the aftermath of the rebellion—it was subsequently noted by Máire Comerford in a personal history of the period that Fitzgerald was amongst the Fianna members who 'had the pleasure of pulling that down and burning it on a dark night during the winter'.

His Military Service Pensions Board file details his subsequent activity in the War of Independence, moving from Na Fianna to the engineers' battalion of the Dublin Brigade of the IRA, before a period of imprisonment that included time in 'Castle, Kilmainham, Arbour Hill and Ballykinlar internment camp'. A brother, Leo Fitzgerald, was killed in a firefight on Brunswick Street in March 1921, on a violent day that claimed thirteen lives in the capital. As a captain in the National Army, Fitzgerald took over the viceregal lodge in 1922, a day on which the press reported that 'the Viceregal Lodge was finally and without question in the possession of the Irish nation'.

RETURN OF THE FLAG
While Fitzgerald sought the return of the Irish Republic flag in his lifetime, and died in March 1962, it would be 1966 before its eventual return to Ireland. At that time the *Irish Independent* told readers that 'who made the flag has never been quite clear' and that the location of the flag subsequently had been 'a mystery'. Neither claim was true. At the British Commonwealth Relations Office, the Irish ambassador, John G. Molloy, received the flag from Sir Saville Garner on 30 March 1966. Taoiseach Seán Lemass said that the presentation of the flag to Ireland was intended 'as a further contribution to the building of better relations and feelings of goodwill between peoples'.

Readers may recall that in 2016 a flag bearing the sunburst emblem of Na Fianna Éireann was temporarily loaned by the Imperial War Museum and exhibited in Dublin's City Hall, where it was noted to have been 'lent by Her Majesty the Queen'. Seized in a raid on Surrey House in the aftermath of the rebellion, the flag includes the legend *Glaine ár gcroí, Neart ár ngéag, Agus beart de réir ár mbriathar* ('Clean in heart, strength in our limbs, and action according to our word'). Little is known of the painting of this flag, or whether Theobald Wolfe Tone Fitzgerald was involved in its making.

Today, the Irish Republic flag is displayed permanently at the National Museum of Ireland, Collins Barracks. Theobald Wolfe Tone was much evoked in the Golden Jubilee celebrations of the Easter Rising, as were the United Irishmen more broadly. Guy Beiner notes, for example, that 'the choice to hold a parade with a contingent of IRA veterans at Toomebridge in 1966 drew a symbolic parallel between commemorations of 1798 and 1916'. By going to the site of the execution of United Irishmen like Roddy McCorley, or by evoking Tone in the pageantry and performance that surrounded the year, a historical connection was being drawn.

TONES, EMMETS AND DE VALERAS

The tradition of naming children in honour of martyrs continued in the aftermath of the centenary year. Abraham William Briscoe, a native of Lithuania who had immigrated to Dublin in the late nineteenth century (at a time when a district of the city would become synonymous with Jewish migration, later earning the moniker of 'Little Jerusalem'), would name a son Wolfe Tone Briscoe in 1900, while his older son—who engaged in significant arms-smuggling during the War of Independence and later served as lord mayor of Dublin—was named Robert Emmet Briscoe.

During and following the revolutionary period, the names of new political martyrs would be bestowed on children. Eamon Morkan, who was still imprisoned for his participation in the Rising at the time, later recalled how 'in October 1916 my wife gave birth to a son, Edward Daly, named after my friend—the Commanding Officer of the 1st Battalion'. In a curious example that shows the far-reaching impacts of the events in Ireland on political consciousness elsewhere, historian Maurice J. Casey has unearthed the case of young Lenin de Valera McKay, christened in Hurst, England, in 1923. 'I call him Lenin', his mother noted, 'because I recognise in Lenin the greatest man of the day … As far as de Valera is concerned … he, in my opinion, in the cause of Ireland and the Movement, is as great a man in his sphere as Lenin.' In the Soviet world, the name Mels served as an acronym of Marx, Engels, Lenin and Stalin.

Eamon Price, present in the Jacob's garrison during the Easter Rising, recalled how after surrender the Volunteers were marched under supervision towards Richmond Barracks, passing 'Lord Edward Street, Thomas Street, past St Catherine's Church, along the *Via Dolorosa* of so many Irish hopes and aspirations'. Some removed their hats, saluting the site of Robert Emmet's execution. For other young men in the revolutionary movement, Emmet and Tone were not only heroes to be idolised but names they carried with them every day.

- *Donal Fallon is Historian in Residence to Dublin City Council Culture Company and the author of* Three castles burning: a history of Dublin in twelve streets *(New Island Books, 2022).*

FURTHER READING

J. Bruck & L. Godson (eds), *Making 1916: material and visual culture of the Easter Rising* (Liverpool, 2015).

M. Hay, *Na Fianna Éireann and the Irish revolution, 1909–23* (Manchester, 2019).

R. Phelan, 'What's up with the Big Green Flag? The conservation of the flag of the Irish Republic' (https://www.flaginstitute.org/wp/wp-content/uploads/2022/11/ICV27-B2-Phelan.pdf).

Below: In the Soviet world, the name Mels served as an acronym of Marx, Engels, Lenin and Stalin.

'BREAKING THE CONNECTION WITH CAPITALISM'—
WOLFE TONE AND THE IRISH REPUBLICAN LEFT

BY **JOHN MULQUEEN**

Above: Liam Mellows—in 'Notes from Mountjoy', written just before his execution in 1922, he wrote that 'We are back to Tone—and it is just as well—relying on that great body "the men of no property"'. (Seán Sexton)

'OUR INDEPENDENCE must be had at all hazards, if the men of property will not support us, they must fall: we can support ourselves by the aid of that numerous and respectable class of the community, the men of no property.'

LIAM MELLOWS

Writing from his prison cell during the Civil War, when republicans were condemned by the bishops and the press as 'communists', Liam Mellows used this quotation from Wolfe Tone's journals to highlight the social-radical character of the United Irishmen and to identify the constituency to which republicans should appeal. In 'Notes from Mountjoy', Mellows wrote that 'We are back to Tone—and it is just as well—relying on that great body "the men of no property". The "stake in the country" people were never with the Republic.' Writing about the 'cult of Tone', Marianne Elliott argues that his 'men of no property' phrase has been 'much misunderstood', but the left-wing republicans who were inspired by Mellows's use of this celebrated phrase knew what Tone meant.

Mellows, at the centre of the study circle in Mountjoy, understood that the IRA needed to promote an economic policy with which workers and small farmers could identify. Dáil Éireann's 'Democratic Programme', socialist in tone, should, in Mellows's words, be 'translated into something definite' to keep 'the workers' on the side of the Republic. Peadar O'Donnell, close to the fledgling Communist Party of Ireland, helped Mellows in the writing of his document, which drew heavily on James Connolly. It was smuggled out, the Free State authorities got their hands on it and the *Irish Independent* publicised the contents of this 'communistic' manifesto in September 1922. One evening in December, after participating in a debate on women in the workforce, O'Donnell wished Mellows a good night. He woke in the morning to hear that Mellows had been shot in what became a series of State-sanctioned extra-legal killings. O'Donnell avoided this fate and was later interned in the Curragh.

FRANK RYAN

Frank Ryan, another Curragh internee, came into his own in the late 1920s as a propagandist and public speaker. He represented the IRA at an anti-imperialist conference in Brussels, which led to the Soviet-sponsored League Against Imperialism, and came home convinced that Ireland's struggle was at one with that of subject peoples around the world. Editor of *An Phoblacht*, Ryan ran a series on Daniel O'Connell and 'Catholic Emancipation' during the centenary year of 1929. Wanting to keep religion out of politics, he cast Tone as his hero against the Catholic O'Connell. Peadar O'Donnell played a leading role in the creation of the IRA's Saor Éire programme, whereby the IRA aimed to provide 'revolutionary leadership' for the—property-less—working class and small farmers to overthrow 'British Imperialism and its ally, Irish Capitalism'. This initiative in 1931 was denounced by the Catholic Church as 'sinful and irreligious', and also by many republicans, such as Mary MacSwiney. New repressive measures came into force, and Cosgrave banned the IRA and the Communist Party. Working together, Church and State knocked out Saor Éire. Unhappy with the IRA leadership's lurch to the right in the wake of this onslaught, Ryan and Hanna Sheehy-Skeffington resigned from *An Phoblacht* in 1933. Catholic militants now took their lead from various church sermons to harass 'communists'. A mob numbering several thousand assembled outside the Communist Party's headquarters, Connolly House, and eventually burned it down; its defenders included left-wing IRA members.

REPUBLICAN CONGRESS

Having won two general elections, Éamon de Valera's Fianna Fáil attracted increasing numbers of republicans away from the IRA. In pursuit of a strategy, along the lines of 'Notes from Mountjoy', O'Donnell and Ryan, with others, believed that a Republican Congress should act as

HISTORY IRELAND/ **71**

WOLFE TONE AND THE IRISH REPUBLICAN LEFT

Above: Frank Ryan of the Republican Congress giving a speech in College Green in 1932. (NLI)

Below: 'Break the connection with capitalism'—the Connolly Workers' Group from Belfast's Shankill Road at Bodenstown in 1934.

a coordinating organisation or umbrella for all 'anti-imperialist' forces representing those without 'a stake in the country'. Following Tone's dictum on eliminating sectarian divisions, the Congress leaders, expelled from the IRA, had some success in gaining a hearing within the Protestant working class in Belfast. The IRA's Bodenstown commemoration in 1934 was notable for the participation of communists and Congress—which, importantly, included a Connolly Workers' Group comprised of Belfast Protestants. The organisers, however, worried about association with socialism, took fright at slogans such as one from the Shankill Road, 'Break the connection with capitalism'. IRA Volunteers, under orders, attempted to seize 'unauthorised' banners, and blows were exchanged. 'Bodenstown', Seán Cronin writes, 'has not witnessed a more ironic scene: Catholics attacking Protestants trying to honour Wolfe Tone and the newspapers made the most of it.' Unsurprisingly, given the overwhelming odds it faced, this left-wing republican project did not survive.

SPANISH CIVIL WAR

When the Catholic hierarchy urged support for the generals who rebelled against Spain's elected government in 1936, Ryan challenged Cardinal Joseph MacRory. In a letter published in the *Irish Times*, he linked the struggle for the Irish Republic and the defence of the Spanish Republic. MacRory wanted the rebels to win because the Catholic Church would be destroyed if they lost. Ryan stated: 'I recall that exactly the same fears were expressed by dignitaries of the Church during our armed struggle for freedom here. Because of that

Above: Cardinal Joseph MacRory (centre)—in 1936 Frank Ryan denounced MacRory's support for the generals who rebelled against Spain's elected government. (Catholic Archives Catalogue)

fear, Irish Republican soldiers were outlawed as "murderers and looters", dubbed "Reds" who would destroy religion, and put under the dire penalties of excommunication.' Had this come to pass? 'I maintain that the real enemies of Christianity in Spain are the Fascist generals who openly proclaim that they will set up a military dictatorship, suppress trade unions and prohibit the workers' right to strike.' The Church should stay out of political affairs, Ryan maintained, and finished this letter with a memorable phrase of his own: 'I will take my politics neither from Moscow nor Maynooth'. At the cardinal's suggestion, Eoin O'Duffy raised more than 700 Catholic ultras to join the notorious Spanish Foreign Legion. The Irish republican left responded by recruiting a smaller number to fight under Ryan with the International Brigades.

A well-attended meeting of republicans in Dublin heard that the *Irish Independent*—'more pro-Franco than Franco himself'—misrepresented Irish opinion in presenting the war in Spain as a conflict over the Church. The *Independent* responded in an editorial, 'The insolence of a clique', and claimed that Irish republicanism could not be compared to 'anti-God' communism. Opposing Wolfe Tone's anti-sectarian doctrine, the editorial spuriously equated republicans with Catholic nationalists: 'The cause of an Irish republic is the cause of an Ireland not merely free but Catholic'. In February the following year Fine Gael aligned itself with the Church, and Franco, when it condemned de Valera's adherence to the international non-intervention policy. Non-intervention, James Dillon claimed, involved 'some measure of sympathy' with the Spanish Republic, where Moscow's agents worked for 'the destruction of Christianity'.

Three months later, republicans criticised de Valera's proposed constitution. Hanna Sheehy-Skeffington argued that it was anti-republican in depriving women of the equal status and opportunities accorded them. She wrote that the Proclamation of the Republic, with its explicit guarantee of equal citizenship, was being scrapped 'for a fascist model', where women were relegated to 'permanent inferiority' as 'the weaker sex'. She pointed out that Connolly had been an early supporter in Ireland of women's rights and had backed the suffragettes 'heart and soul'. For Rosamond Jacob, a historian of the United Irishmen, de Valera was simply 'too damn Catholic'. Frank Ryan, back in Dublin to recover from the wounds he had sustained in Spain, alluded to Tone's 'men of no property' phrase when he condemned the draft constitution as one that enthroned 'the power of the rich' over 'the plain people'. Peadar O'Donnell contended that the draft was the 'triumph' of the Griffith school of nationalism over the teachings of 'Tone, Lalor, Mitchel, Pearse, Connolly and Mellows'. The Catholic bishops would receive a privileged place in the Irish state as 'the watchdogs' of private property.

Shortly before he was captured by Italian troops in 1938, Ryan wrote that his Irish unit fought and died in Spain to restore 'a historical connection with the international struggle that existed in the time of the United Irishmen'. Four months earlier, in a Radio Madrid talk, he had developed this point:

'I recall that when we came here first, a leading Irish newspaper—in an effort not to be too harsh on us—depicted us as idealists who went to fight other people's battles, thereby implying that we are avoiding fighting our own. No interpretation could be more incorrect. We are realists. In the task of freeing Ireland in our generation where was initiative shown if not from men like Kit Conway, Charley Donnelly, William Beattie, Peter Daly and scores of other Irishmen whose graves are today on the battlefields of Spain? Just as these had the correct conception of a free Ireland—the conception of Tone, of Connolly, of Mellows—so they had a correct conception of Ireland's place on the earth.'

BRENDAN BEHAN

In 1939 left-wing republicans in London launched *Irish Freedom* (later the *Irish Democrat*) as a monthly paper pitched at Britain's Irish community. It eulogised Connolly and Mellows, and covered trade union issues and independence struggles across the British Empire. It also followed the Moscow line on Nazi Germany, as did the few Irish communists imprisoned alongside IRA members during the war. Writing from Mountjoy in 1942, Brendan Behan concluded that the militarist IRA was 'defunct' because it had no popular appeal. This politically aware republican found that he did not have much in common with his comrades, quite a few of whom had no issue with O'Duffy. While most of them were 'sincere and honest', they were not actually republicans. Behan expressed support for the communist position on the war:

'Britain and the US should open the second front to ease the pressure on the Soviet Union. In the Curragh, Michael O'Riordan, who fought with the International Brigades, opposed any reliance by the IRA on Germany based on the

HISTORY IRELAND/ 73

Above: Brendan Behan outside the High Court, Dublin, in 1961. Writing from Mountjoy in 1942, he concluded that many of his IRA comrades, while 'sincere and honest', were not actually republicans.

simplistic principle that "England's difficulty is Ireland's opportunity". He employed Terence MacSwiney's argument that if Ireland were to obtain its liberty at the expense of other peoples, it would deserve all the execration she herself poured on tyranny throughout the ages.'

Another internee in the communist-led Connolly Group, Jim Savage, began his political education by reading James Connolly but moved on to Karl Marx with *The Communist Manifesto*. After his release he joined the Labour Party, a shelter of sorts for communists in de Valera's Ireland from 1941 to 1944. Savage worked with O'Riordan in a new Labour branch named after Liam Mellows, where they quickly ran into trouble in that timid, if not conservative, party.

COLD WAR
The onset of the Cold War gave a new impetus to Ireland's anti-communist zealots. Following the imprisonment in 1946 of Archbishop Aloysius Stepinac in Yugoslavia, the Dáil unanimously condemned Tito's action. Hubert Butler attempted to draw attention to Stepinac's role in the Croatian fascist regime during the war but was pilloried in the press for his efforts. He then faced a systematic ostracism campaign in his native Kilkenny. John Charles McQuaid, the archbishop of Dublin, made a radio appeal in 1948 for money to combat communism in Italy, and more than £60,000—a considerable sum—was quickly collected to assist the Christian Democrats in Italy's general election; this time no public figure such as Ryan opposed Church interference in politics. The next year 150,000 protested against the imprisonment in Hungary of Cardinal József Mindszenty, resulting in another unanimous condemnation by the Dáil. Hungary's 1956 uprising, and the subsequent Soviet invasion, again saw publicly expressed anti-communism, when the *Irish Independent* promoted a Mindszenty personality cult. Behan, however, remained loyal to the Soviet cause. In a letter to the *Daily Worker* in London, he wrote that he too had been upset at the spectacle of Red Army tanks in Budapest, but he had not yet fallen for 'the lies of our enemies' in Ireland, such as those published by the *Independent*; in 1916 that paper called for the blood of 'the bravest and best' and 'applauded the murder of the seventy-seven in 1922'. Behan, until recently a man of no property, now a successful writer, apologised for not signing his letter; he had a play running in the Abbey. He concluded by writing that the Hungary crisis had served to unite communists in Dublin; 'the boys will remember Connolly House which we defended (I was a Fianna boy under the late Frank Ryan then) in 1933'.

WOLFE TONE SOCIETIES
From 1962, following the failure of its 'border campaign', the leadership of what Billy McMillen termed 'a broken IRA' began to emphasise socialism, secularism and anti-sectarianism. This departure, Ultán Gillen writes, was rooted in republican teaching, 'especially the Marxism of James Connolly and the foundational ideas of Theobald Wolfe Tone, particularly Tone's belief that overcoming sectarianism was the means to revolutionary change in Ireland'. Symbolically, in September 1963, during a series of lectures marking the bicentenary of Tone's birth, Cathal Goulding, the IRA chief of staff, invited Hubert Butler, a Protestant, to speak in the Mansion House on 'The ideology of Tone'. This focused on what Butler described as Tone's 'imperishable ideal', the common name of Irishman. The bicentenary events led to the formation of Wolfe Tone Societies in Dublin, Belfast and Cork, whose object, founding member Seán Cronin remembered, was to create 'some kind of bridge to, at least, some Protestant intellectuals in the North through discussions, seminars, lectures. The society did not achieve a great deal, but it was a meeting place for republicans, socialists, communists, Irish language revivalists, and it developed new ideas.'

Times had changed, and the republican left no longer had to fear the bishops—'the belt of the crozier'. The IRA began to co-operate with the Communist Party in various agitations, particularly the provision of public housing and, most significantly, civil rights in the North. What did national independence mean? The answer, according to left-wing republicans, was the *ownership* of Ireland. Seán Garland addressed the 1968 Bodenstown commemoration to highlight how the IRA's political wing could lead the revolutionary struggle for independence. He invoked Tone and Mellows in specifying which class would support this, 'the men of no property'.

> 'one is now expected to be more conversant with the thoughts of Chairman Mao than those of our dead Patriots.'

AN ALIEN IDEOLOGY?

Bringing Irish republicanism into the broader 'anti-imperialist' world of the 1960s involved asking questions of cherished customs. When Roy Johnston, an independently minded communist, criticised the recitation of the Rosary at republican commemorations, he offended at least one leading traditionalist, Seán Mac Stíofáin. But linking Tone and, for example, Mellows in republican rhetoric did not blind some of the IRA's old guard to what they saw as a Marxist—'alien'—influence over Goulding's cohort. In 1969 the Belfast veteran Jimmy Steele alleged that 'one is now expected to be more conversant with the thoughts of Chairman Mao than those of our dead Patriots'.

Garland later responded to these charges of an 'alien' influence in his next speech at Bodenstown, two and a half years after the 1969–70 split in the republican movement. 'We have been accused of adopting an alien ideology', he began, but the opponents of Goulding's 'new departure' would find the inspiration of the French Revolution 'in all that Tone wrote'. The Irish 'revolutionary party', Garland continued, should be proud of its internationalism. 'If it is alien to recognise the common humanity of working people struggling for freedom everywhere in the world, then call us alien and be damned.' With the Official IRA on ceasefire, in June 1973 McMillen warned his audience at Bodenstown that republicans did not stand 'on the brink of victory' in the North but 'on the brink of sectarian disaster'. Addressing representatives of the French Communist Party at this commemoration, Tomás Mac Giolla recognised that France symbolised 'the internationalism of Tone and the United Irishmen'.

The supporters of the post-split Provisional IRA, led by Mac Stíofáin, could also invoke Tone. In February 1970, just over a year after civil rights marchers were ambushed by cudgel-wielding Protestant ultras—marking, arguably, the beginning of 'the Troubles'—the first issue of a revived *An Phoblacht* declared that Tone had spoken 'for all generations' of republicans. His aim was to 'break the connection with England'. The Provisionals repudiated 'Free Stateism and all other isms' not in line with 'traditional Republican and Separatist policy', but the 'traditionalists' who pursued a militarist IRA strategy were gradually elbowed aside by a left-wing cohort led by Gerry Adams. In Long Kesh, Adams directed a republican education programme and urged the prisoners to ground their reading in the Irish tradition: read Che Guevara and Ho Chi Minh, but Connolly and Mellows are closer to home.

In his Bodenstown address in 1983 Adams, by then the Sinn Féin MP for West Belfast, argued that a political movement was required, particularly in the South, to complement the IRA's 'armed resistance to the British presence'. 'We can be assured if Wolfe Tone were alive today, he would be with us', but he would also be vilified, Adams suggested, 'as an upstart, a subversive and the 1798 equivalent of a gunman. He would even be banned from RTÉ.' Sinn Féin made its own 'anti-imperialist' alliances. When the ANC's Nelson Mandela visited Dublin in 1990, he endorsed Adams's then controversial proposal for talks between Sinn Féin and the British government on the conflict in the North.

Frank Ryan's remains were repatriated from East Germany in 1979 and buried in Glasnevin cemetery; all strands of Irish republicanism, constitutional and revolutionary, were represented at the funeral. Thirty-six years later the Sinn Féin mayor of Belfast, Arder Carson, unveiled a stained-glass window in City Hall to commemorate the Belfast *brigadistas*, from the Falls and the Shankill, who fought for the Spanish Republic. Almost a century earlier, on 20 June 1922, on behalf of the Four Courts garrison, Liam Mellows made a prophetic statement at Bodenstown. Those remembering Tone on that day had not come to 'sing the swansong' of Irish republicanism; 'though the outlook was black and the odds against them heavy', they would stay on the straight road, believing 'their cause was just'. Mellows and Ryan, and their adherents, followed Wolfe Tone in the cause of liberty. As Hubert Butler understood, however, the challenge that Tone bequeathed the nation remains—substituting for 'Protestant, Catholic and Dissenter' the common name of Irishman.

- *John Mulqueen is currently working on a study of Frank Ryan and his political world, 1932–45.*

FURTHER READING

S. Cronin, *Frank Ryan: the search for the Republic* (Dublin, 1980).

U. Gillen, 'Theobald Wolfe Tone and the common name of Irishman in 1960s Ireland', in S. Paseta (ed.), *Uncertain futures: essays about the Irish past for Roy Foster* (Oxford, 2016).

J. Mulqueen, *'An alien ideology': Cold War perceptions of the Irish republican left* (Liverpool, 2022).

C.J. Woods, *Bodenstown revisited: the grave of Theobald Wolfe Tone, its monuments and its pilgrimages* (Dublin, 2018).

CONOR CRUISE O'BRIEN'S TONE—AN EXCEPTIONAL CASE?

BY MARION KELLY

Above: Conor Cruise O'Brien *c*. 1968—despite his status as arch-revisionist, he was unwilling to undermine Tone's status as an enlightened secular democrat.

CONOR CRUISE O'BRIEN wrote extensively on subjects that arise in any consideration of Wolfe Tone's political commitments, such as the nature of political legitimacy and when, and whether, violence can be justified. He also drew heavily on Edmund Burke, whose *Reflections on the Revolution in France* is regarded as a canonical counter-revolutionary tract. Why, then, does Tone feature so infrequently in O'Brien's writing? One would imagine that such a seminal figure in Irish history, who inspired generations of Irish republicans, would be a more vivid presence therein. O'Brien was compelled by schismatic events, and the French Revolution was a paradigmatic tool in his interpretive framework. His analysis of Thomas Jefferson hinges largely on Jefferson's early unqualified support for the French Revolution, with a particular emphasis on Jefferson's refrain that 'The tree of liberty must be refreshed from time to time with the blood of patriots and tyrants', yet Tone's presence in revolutionary France in order to raise support for an Irish expeditionary force elicits relatively minor treatment. O'Brien, it appears, despite his status as arch-revisionist, was unwilling to undermine Tone's status as an enlightened secular democrat—unlike Tom Dunne, who questioned Tone's ideological motivations in *Theobald Wolfe Tone: colonial outsider* (part of what Marianne Elliot has referred to as a new trend of defrocking Irish nationalist mythology in her review of his work).

THE BELL

O'Brien's first significant political intervention was at the annual national conference of the Irish Labour Party in 1936, as a delegate from Trinity College. He broke with procedural rules and condemned Franco's aggression in Spain. When he was heckled for being from Trinity, he defended himself by noting that all progressive movements in the country over the last 150 years had their origins in Trinity College, citing Wolfe Tone, Robert Emmet and Thomas Davis.

O'Brien cut his teeth in writing in early contributions to *The Bell*, a fact that aligned him with contemporary republican engagement in the post-Civil War period. The first editorial of *The Bell* was living proof that a republican background was no obstacle to inclusivity, ending with the declaration that *The Bell* excluded no one—all readers were welcomed, 'Gentile or Jew, Protestant or Catholic, priest or layman, Big House or Small House'—and as such would prove attractive to those feeling that the version of republicanism in which they believed had been hijacked by republicanism in name only. O'Brien, as a fledgling scholar and critic, was undoubtedly influenced by Seán O'Faolain's pronouncements and priorities.

Above: Thomas Jefferson—O'Brien's analysis of him hinges largely on Jefferson's early unqualified support for the French Revolution.

The cultural regeneration that *The Bell* advocated warranted reflection, and this was fertile ground for those seeking new ways of understanding history. O'Faolain led the way in that endeavour, writing a number of biographies of historical figures who loomed large in the Irish nationalist historical imagination. Maurice Harmon reflected that those whom O'Faolain chose to reconfigure historically, and imaginatively, were creative individuals, 'living at a time of great social change, at a pivotal moment in history, and capable of meeting that change effectively'. Yet in *The Irish* O'Faolain characterised 'Men like Tone, Mitchel, Doheny' as 'smothered talents', who had deprived themselves, 'and Ireland, of as much as they gave' and who had choked 'the critical side of their minds'. O'Faolain concluded that 'they were good rebels in proportion as they were bad revolutionaries, so that their passion for change and their vision of change never pierced to organic change, halted dead at the purely modal and circumstantial'. Reflecting on this time in *Vive moi*, O'Faolain came to see much of his former idealism as an aberration of character. Daniel Corkery's belief that 'All idealists are callous' resonated with O'Faolain's interpretation of his own experience of blind idealism as a time when he quickly became 'heartless, humourless, and pitiless'.

O'Brien was circumstantially primed for this exegesis on the nature of commitment to abstractions such as Faith and Fatherland, coming from a family whose fate was bound up with the form these abstractions took in Irish rhetoric and political life. He would, in time, run the gauntlet of criticism for his relentless adherence to an idea that O'Faolain was working out in the aftermath of his earlier commitments—an adherence that became more relentless as O'Brien's career progressed. O'Faolain's pronouncements are noteworthy in that they prefigure O'Brien's later imaginative and critical tendency to use the French Revolution as a comparative device, or a herald of sorts. O'Faolain had noted Matthew Arnold's suggestion that the French Revolution had its source 'in a great movement of feeling, not in a great movement of mind'. This reinforced O'Faolain's belief that Irish rebels 'devoted their lives and all their beings to passion rather than to thought'. His notion that Irish rebels had primarily seized 'upon the emotional content' and not the 'intellectual content' of revolution was a strain of thought that O'Brien would eventually harness to his own ends.

SHIFT IN O'BRIEN'S POLITICS

By 1999 O'Brien was to commend de Valera's policy of internment during the Second World War in terms that summon precisely the oppositional thinking he had cultivated in his linking of the progress of Irish politics to the characters and symbolism of the French Revolution. O'Brien recollects asking de Valera whether he had been influenced by Edmund Burke, to which de Valera replied 'Of course not, Burke was *not a Republican*'. O'Brien comments that, 'in spite of that non sequitur, his mind was more like Burke's than Tone's. This, of course, meant that I liked Dev.'

Below: Edmund Burke—O'Brien's attraction to Burke culminated in his 1992 biography, *The great melody*. (NGI)

CONOR CRUISE O'BRIEN'S TONE—AN EXCEPTIONAL CASE?

O'Brien's attraction to Edmund Burke culminated in his biography of Burke, *The great melody*, but it was a long and slow-burning affair that transcended what some commentators have perceived as a shift in his politics. In 1969, when O'Brien was being fêted by the Left internationally as the poster boy of post-colonialism, he published a collection of essays, *The suspecting glance*. Burke's scepticism of human nature and his cautionary tone pervade the essays, explicitly at the level of content but perhaps more significantly in the clear message that a suspecting glance was what was called for. O'Brien's essays arose out of the content of a course he taught in New York University on 'Literature and Society'. His criticism of American neo-imperialism and his active involvement in the protest movement against the Vietnam War made his course highly attractive to left-wing students and activists. Yet, he tells us, he felt disconcerted by their cheerful talk of revolution, 'without any trace of awe or compunction at the thought of what such a revolution—if it became possible—would mean in terms of human suffering, including their own suffering'. He was to disconcert them in turn. Instead of teaching Herbert Marcuse or even Percy Bysshe Shelley, 'I went on endlessly about Edmund Burke, a thinker to whom no spontaneous inclination of their own would ever have drawn them'. He made the significance of the French Revolution in his own schema palpably clear when he wrote that:

'There is a real sense in which the cold war can be said to have begun in November 1790, with the publication of Edmund Burke's *Reflections on the Revolution in France*. Ever since that date, the idea of revolution has been an important factor in our intellectual life: fear of it, or hope of it, produced contrasting mental anthologies from reality, contrasting styles and theologies, dreams and nightmares.'

The last line is evocative of 1798, and the impact of the French Revolution closer to home. In an article in the *New York Review of Books*, published in 1986, O'Brien describes Tone as 'one of a number of European *patriotes* who during the 1790s—in Belgium, Holland, the Rhineland, and various parts of Italy as well as in Ireland, sought to shake off monarchical, aristocratic, clerical, and/or alien rule and turn their countries into sister republics, *républiques soeurs*, of *la Grande Nation*, Revolutionary France'.

PATRICK PEARSE

O'Brien provides his readership with an analysis of the legacy of 1798 in a review of Tom Wilson's *Ulster: conflict and consent* in 1990. The chief point that he was at pains to make is that Tone had been incorporated into nationalist mythology in a manner that was at odds with Tone's philosophy. In a telling observation, he writes: 'There is an ominous resemblance between the pattern of feelings of modern Catholic Republicans toward Wolfe Tone and Protestants, and the pattern of feelings of traditional Catholics toward Jesus and the Jews. In each case, the great teacher is felt to have been rejected and betrayed by his own people, and then adopted by another people, the Catholics.' In 'Bobby Sands: mutations of nationalism', first published in the *New York Review of Books* in 1986, O'Brien made a distinction between Tone's ideology and that of the Irish republicanism expressed by Patrick Pearse. He writes that Wolfe Tone and his friends 'were militant secularists, deists and atheists, contemptuous of superstition, and especially of Roman Catholic superstition'. He notes that it was 'Tone's ironic fate to become a major saint in the Pearsean Pantheon. The grave of the man who had set out to emancipate his country from superstition had become "the holiest place in Ireland".' In a comical aside, he uses an anthropological illustration to show how Tone's secular republicanism had metamorphosed into Catholic republicanism. On collective farms in Western Siberia shamanism had taken on syncretic forms, 'blending Communist teaching with traditional beliefs'. In this way, the defeated Parisian communards in 1871 took refuge in Lake Baikal, where they were symbolically metamorphosed into otters and modern fishermen offered them as sacrifices to fulfil their quota under the Party's fishery plan. O'Brien wryly observed that 'the metamorphosis of Theobald

Below: Patrick Pearse—in 'Bobby Sands: mutations of nationalism', first published in the *New York Review of Books* in 1986, O'Brien made a distinction between Tone's ideology and that of the Irish republicanism expressed by Pearse. (Pearse Museum)

Wolfe Tone, in the thaumaturgic hands of Patrick Pearse, is hardly less fishy'.

TONE AND BURKE

O'Brien was attuned to the performative nature of politics and worked out his ideas in a wide range of contexts, most notably in his book *UN: sacred drama*. With regard to Burke, his exemplar, he writes: 'Edmund Burke saw the theatre as a school of moral sentiments; he was also in the habit of viewing politics as theatre. His first reaction to news of the French Revolution was the same as to the going up of a curtain: "What spectators and what Actors!".' O'Brien writes that Burke was 'by no means alone in this way of imagining politics' and that 'it is remarkable how the vocabulary of theatre permeates political discussion: "scene", "stage", "role", "scenario", "players", "acts" and "drama" itself are all part of current journalistic and academic terminology in relation to politics.'

This again raises the question of that other Irish exemplar of revolutionary republican struggle, Wolfe Tone, who was both spectator and actor and whose diaries are an abundant resource for anyone interested in piecing together the theatrical and self-consciously stylised new modes of representation *en vogue* in revolutionary-era France, and whose death, in performative terms, has all the hallmarks of a classical republican gesture. Did the fact that Tone shared Burke's concerns for the oppressed majority in Ireland factor in O'Brien's unwillingness to vilify such a clear-cut revolutionary figure? Tone and Burke were united in respect of the appalling indifference and callousness of the Protestant Ascendancy towards the native majority. In Burke's words in 1797, the system of military government was 'mad in the extreme—merely as a system, but still worse in the mad hands in which it is placed'.

O'Brien, drawing on Marianne Elliot, writes in *The great melody* that while the involvement of Burke, the great counter-revolutionary, in the Catholic Committee in its radical phase from 1790 onwards 'may appear a startling paradox', it may not be as surprising as it at first seems. He argues that Burke understood that fear of the spread of Jacobin ideas could be used to further the cause of securing full Catholic enfranchisement. He stresses that while Tone and Burke 'were radically

> ' ... the system of military government was mad in the extreme—merely as a system, but still worse in the mad hands in which it is placed.'
> —Edmund Burke

opposed to each other in respect of the French Revolution', they were allies in respect of both the principle of Catholic enfranchisement 'and the Catholic Committee's programme for securing it, through popular agitation, with an implicit threat [of violence] behind it'. Yet ultimately O'Brien concedes that this is where the meeting of minds ends, as their long-term goals were very far apart.

When O'Brien addresses Tone's hope that the spread of revolutionary activity would destroy sectarian differences and emancipate Ireland from British rule and Catholic superstition, it is with some degree of veneration. He writes in *States of Ireland* that 'I have seen tears in the eyes of an Ulster Catholic Republican when he tried to express what he felt about Wolfe Tone'.

O'Brien's position on Tone was shaped by his understanding of and sympathy towards Tone's circumstances. Had O'Brien been born in Tone's era, in Tone's circumstances, could he have imagined himself acting similarly? There are strong parallels between Tone's instincts as a young man and O'Brien's. In fact, the trajectory of their careers has much in common: both were outsiders of a sort, both gravitated towards contributing to the political establishment of their day, both were highly ambitious, both cut bold figures in Trinity College, both were impassioned advocates of the separation of powers, and neither were in the business of declining a glass of claret when the occasion arose.

Tone was ultimately measured, humane and clear in his understanding of Burke's ability and his motivations. I use the word 'humane' here in connection with a moving passage in Tone's diaries after his meeting with Thomas Paine in Paris. When Tone relayed to Paine the 'shattered state' of Burke's mind after the death of his only son, the latter responded that it was *Rights of man* that had broken his heart and that the death of his son 'gave him occasion to develop the chagrin'. Tone later writes in his diary: 'I am sure the Rights of Man have tormented Burke exceedingly, but I have seen myself the workings of a father's grief upon his spirit, and I could not be deceived. Paine has no children!' This may be an important factor in terms of grasping O'Brien's unwillingness to align Tone with Jean-Jacques Rousseau or Thomas Jefferson, figures that potentially align with Tone in O'Brien's interpretive schema. O'Brien wasn't above the *ad hominem* attack when it served to prove a point, and he quotes Burke's scathing comment on Rousseau's paternal conduct with a notable hint of relish: 'The Bear ... loves, licks and forms her young; but bears are not philosophers'.

- *Marion Kelly completed her Ph.D, 'Between childhood and night'—the role of literature and emotion in the writing of Conor Cruise O'Brien, in the School of English, Trinity College, Dublin.*

FURTHER READING

D.H. Akenson, *Conor: a biography of Conor Cruise O'Brien* (Montreal, 1994).

C. Cruise O'Brien, *States of Ireland* (London, 1972).

C. Cruise O'Brien, *The suspecting glance* (London, 1972).

C. Cruise O'Brien, *The great melody: a thematic biography and commented anthology of Edmund Burke* (London, 1992).

WRITING *WOLFE TONE—PROPHET OF IRISH INDEPENDENCE*

BY **MARIANNE ELLIOTT**

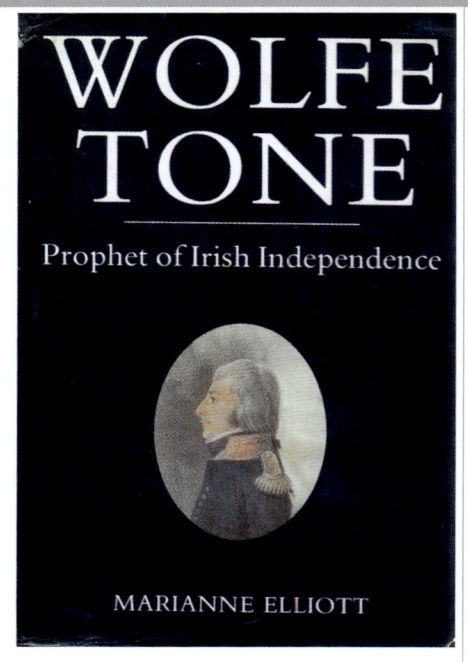

IT IS 35 YEARS SINCE I published my biography of Wolfe Tone. Much to my own surprise, it is still in print. Tone himself was a compulsive writer and he was good at it. I was struck by how little scoring out there is in his original writings, even in his influential *Argument on behalf of the Catholics of Ireland*, written in under two days in 1791 and credited with bringing about the formation of the Society of United Irishmen. Initially, however, it resulted in his appointment as secretary and agent to the Catholic Committee, and even after he had been forced into exile and started to become the republican of legend it was his time as Catholic agent that he reflected on most. He was more than the plaster saint of militant republicanism. Part of the joy, and burden, of writing a biography is that the subject becomes part of your life, an obsession. How fortunate I was to have had such a figure as Theobald Wolfe Tone to obsess about, and one who, two and a half centuries on, still finds such a wide public audience.

As an undergraduate at Queen's University, Belfast, I always knew that I wanted to work on the United Irishmen. It had been a particular obsession of my father's; he carried it into the theatre, playing a number of roles in the plays of the legendary Tommy Carnduff. I was blessed to have studied with Jim Beckett and Peter Jupp at Queen's University, and latterly to have befriended A.T.Q. Stewart. I also studied French at Queen's and knew that I had the tools to use the French archives, without which it would have been impossible to tell the full story of Tone. I spoke with the head of department, Professor Michael Roberts, about my hope of doing a Ph.D on the United Irishmen and France, and thought that TCD and R.B. McDowell might be the most suitable destination. 'No, my dear', I recall him saying. 'I know exactly where you should go.' He contacted the Oxford-based Richard Cobb—one of the top French Revolutionary scholars in the world—and the course of my life was changed forever, for in Oxford I met my husband Trevor.

HUISSIERS AND LEGIONNAIRES

It was also via Oxford and the French History network that I won a French government scholarship, enabling me to live in Paris and access the many archives that contained Tone's correspondence and memoranda for the French government. I was also fortunate to visit former Irish senator and founding member of Fine Gael Frank MacDermott there. He was a gracious and generous man who had written a pioneering work on Tone in 1939. The French archives could be intimidating for the uninitiated. In those days the *huissiers* who delivered your orders ruled supreme. They could decide how long you had to wait for your documents and sometimes would not deliver them at all. Then there were the war and naval archives, operated by the armed services. They were located in the Château de Vincennes, also the headquarters of the French Foreign Legion. After having to run the gauntlet of the *legionnaires*, one faced intimidating interrogation by the soldier overseeing the research room.

If, however, you were lucky enough to be taken on board by the archivists—a class of people to whom I owe so much—their generosity opened many doors. One day in the *salle des inventaires* at the Archives Nationales, an elegant middle-aged woman leaned over and asked why I was so interested in the papers covering the 1796 Bantry Bay invasion attempt on Ireland. After I explained, she took me under her wing. She was cataloguing related papers, and on the weekends and public holidays, when the archives were otherwise closed, she brought me into the inner sanctuary, where I had free reign to pull my chosen documents off the shelves—oh joy, no *huissiers* to placate—a researcher's dream. But most of all it housed the legendary police archives that Richard Cobb had talked about so much and used so effectively. These were the records of the feared police established by the Committee of General Security under the Terror. In the precursor to those intimidating questionnaires that every occupant of even lowly hostelries in France had to complete until recent years, the

Above: Archibald Hamilton Rowan, another United Irish exile—a year before Tone's arrival in Paris in February 1796 he had barely escaped the guillotine.

police monitored where foreigners lived in Paris. The results survived in the chits of paper organised into tiny bundles on floor-to-ceiling shelving to which I was now given access in the back of the Archives Nationales. Through these I was able to trace the addresses of all the United Irishmen who ended up as exiles in Paris, including Tone. On Sundays, when the archives were closed, I would walk Paris, mapping his time there.

'A WAR, NOT AN INSURRECTION'

Tone had been exiled to America in 1795. It might surprise Irish-Americans how much he hated the country. Indeed, his almost fanatical criticisms could be read as culturally élitist. Americans simply did not know their place! One senses real relief when he arrived in France in February 1796, pursuing the agreement with his United Irish friends that he would use his enforced exile to negotiate French aid to secure Irish independence from Britain. A

> **'I do not desire to have the blood even of the wicked upon me'**

new regime, the Directory, had replaced the Terror—mercifully for him, as the previous year another United Irish exile, Archibald Hamilton Rowan, had barely escaped the guillotine. Tone frowned upon the Terror, its Revolutionary Tribunal and terrifying police committee. He was distressed at the sight of the Temple prison, where Louis XVI had been held. His request that the French send a large force to Ireland was determined by his dislike of bloodshed. He wanted 'a war, not an insurrection', and hoped that even the aristocrats who opposed them might be spared and permitted to emigrate to England: 'for I am like Parson Adams in Fielding's *Joseph Andrews*, I do not desire to have the blood even of the wicked upon me'.

Tone's tactic from the outset had been to remain almost totally isolated to preserve secrecy. Yet he did not relish such isolation, and his loneliness is palpable in his journal entries. For days on end he was forced to be a tourist, but in the heavy snows of March 1796 Paris looked melancholy. He would sit alone for hours in the cafés. Discussion with (and admiration by) like minds had been a key element in his success as a political writer in Ireland. 'Am I not to be sincerely pitied here?', he wrote on 29 March. 'I do not know a soul! I speak the language but with great difficulty! I live in Taverns, which I

WRITING *WOLFE TONE—PROPHET OF IRISH INDEPENDENCE*

Above: With Kay Dickason (right), great-great granddaughter of Wolfe Tone. Note on the shelf behind her the original miniature of Tone painted by his granddaughter, which Kay gave me permission to use on my dust-jacket.

detest! … I return to my apartment … as if I was returning to gaol, and finally I go to bed at night as if I was mounting the guillotine—I do lead a dog's life of it here that is the truth of it.' Tone's Paris journals are full of his insecurities and little of that social confidence that made his company so coveted in Dublin and Belfast. He was always short of money, and even when his negotiations began to bear fruit and invasion plans were progressing he was forced to borrow from his friend and patron James Monroe, American minister to France and future president. He occasionally reflects on his own position if the invasion should succeed. He recalls Thomas Russell foretelling great things for him and permits himself some fleeting pride, but he quickly dismisses the idea even of being Irish ambassador to France. 'When a government was formed in Ireland it would be time enough to talk of embassies.' Most people only know Tone through his *Life*/autobiography, written as he awaited posting with Hoche's force in 1796 and very heavily edited by his widow and son, and I felt that it could only be understood in the context of his other contemporary activities and writings while in France.

KAY DICKASON, TONE'S GREAT-GREAT-GRANDDAUGHTER

After publication of a first book, *Partners in revolution: the United Irishmen and France* (1982), I was already considering writing about Tone when something extraordinary happened. It was spring 1984. I had been teaching at the University of South Carolina and took advantage of spring break to visit the Library of Congress in Washington. Tone's son had married the daughter of United Irishman and exile to America William Sampson. It was his papers that I had travelled to see. 'Would you like to know who made them available to the library?', the archivist asked me. 'I'm sure she would like to hear from you.' This would turn out to be Kay Dickason, great-great granddaughter of Wolfe Tone. And the archivist was right. She responded by return and invited me to her home in Short Hills, New Jersey, the first of many visits until she died in 1995 at the age of 92. Thus began a wonderful friendship. Kay was a remarkable woman, clever, with an irreverent wit and remarkable recall of family oral history. Because Tone's widow, Matilda, lived to old age, I learnt from Kay family traditions passed through her father, Lascelles Chester Maxwell, and grandmother, Grace Georgiana Tone Maxwell, Tone's only grandchild. The sociability of Tone and Matilda's household had descended through the generations and Kay would share the family's history with me during the pre-dinner cocktail hour (yes, cocktails), with Kay changing into evening wear for the occasion. It was from her that I learnt about the strength of character of Tone's wife, Matilda. She would need it, given how her life worked out. After eloping with Tone at the age of sixteen—he was 22—there were long periods of separation, two years when he attended the Inns of Court in the 1780s and over a year after he left

America for France in 1796.

Best of all, Kay gave me access to Tone's and Matilda's papers, which generations from Matilda down to herself had preserved. She was critical of her aunt for giving some original papers away—those in the Library of Congress were microfilm copies—while those gifted to the American-Irish Historical Library in New York had disappeared when Kay and I went to find them. Did they ever reappear? She was also well aware of the loss of a trunkful of papers that Matilda Tone had confided to their friend Dr James Reynolds when she and the children sailed from America to rejoin Tone in 1797. They may have contained the letters he wrote during his long residence in London in 1787–8. Matilda told her granddaughter, Grace Georgiana (1 March 1848), that she received 'constant letters' from Tone during his time at the Middle Temple. They have never resurfaced.

I would rise early and go down to the basement before our walk with Kay's dog. No waiting on the whims of *huissiers* here! Surrounded by Tone memorabilia—including the original miniature of Tone painted by his granddaughter and which Kay gave me permission to use on my dust-jacket—it was not difficult to be transported back to those times. Here were Tone's letters to Matilda, to key figures in France and elsewhere, as well as to friends, in the lead-up to the Bantry Bay expedition, during his roving mission as General Hoche's aide-de-camp through France, Germany and the Netherlands, the frustrating preparation for another Irish invasion attempt in 1797 and his final days preparing to embark again for Ireland after the 1798 rebellion. On each occasion, as he was boarding ship as part of French attempts to invade Ireland, he would prepare Matilda for his possible death.

TONE'S FINAL LETTERS TO MATILDA
He wrote two final letters to Matilda on 10 November 1798. One uses the French revolutionary calendar, 20 Brumaire an 7.

'Dearest Love,

The hour is at last come, when we must part: as no words can express what I feel for you and our children, I shall not attempt it;—complaint of any kind would be beneath your courage or mine; be assured I will die as I have lived, and that you will have no reason to blush for me.

I have written on your behalf to the French government … and to those of my friends who are about to go into exile, and who I am sure will not abandon you.

Adieu, Dearest Love, I find it impossible to finish this letter; give my Love to Mary [his sister] and above all things remember that you are now the only parent of our dearest children, and that the best proof you can give of your affection for me, will be to preserve yourself for their education—God almighty bless you all,
Yours ever, TW Tone.'

The second one, later that day, assured Matilda that her own family, her brother Edward and sister Harriet, had promised him that they would do everything to assist and protect her. They never did. It concludes: 'Adieu, Dearest Love; Keep your courage, as I have kept mine; my mind is as tranquil this moment as at any period of my life; cherish my memory, and especially preserve your health and spirits for the sake of our dearest Children. Your ever affectionate, TW Tone.' My sidenotes on reading the originals of these in Kay's basement are that they were written in a 'very firm hand'.

Tone's closest friends, particularly Thomas Russell, were already by this time prisoners elsewhere in Dublin. From Newgate Russell tried to save him and undoubtedly would have moved mountains to help his widow, but he and the other State prisoners were detained in Fort George in Scotland until the 1802 Amiens peace treaty with France. Russell was executed in 1803, having returned to Ireland to help organise Emmet's rebellion. The British government would have been happy to grant their wish of exile to America in 1798 had not the American minister in London, Rufus King—with the approval of US President John Adams—refused. When these United Irish leaders finally made it to America in 1804–5, Thomas Addis Emmet and William James MacNevin had their revenge, thwarting King's campaign to be elected for New York state in 1807.

SQUABBLING UNITED IRISH EXILES
They did also support and keep in regular touch with Matilda, particularly in the campaign to revive Tone's reputation in Ireland. The last year of Tone's life was blighted by squabbles among the United Irish exiles in France. Tone hated nastiness and dissension and, as Matilda would confirm, would often walk away from it. The remarkable success of his French mission in 1796 owed not a little to the fact that he acted alone, and his talents were quickly recognised by the French Directory. When exiles from the failed 1798 rebellion started to flood into France, the egregious Napper Tandy led the faction aggrieved that the French government continued to see Tone as United Irish spokesperson.

Above: James Napper Tandy—when exiles from the failed 1798 rebellion started to flood into France, he led the faction aggrieved that the French government continued to see Tone as United Irish spokesperson. (*Cox's Irish Magazine*/TCD)

WRITING WOLFE TONE—PROPHET OF IRISH INDEPENDENCE

Above: 'Tone's Interview with Napoleon, December 23, 1797'. Napoleon thought well of Tone. It was the personal intervention of the Bonaparte family that secured Matilda a pension. (*Weekly Freeman and National Press*, 11 December 1897/NLI)

Matilda was furious, particularly at their efforts to harness his reputation after his death when they had sought to undermine him in life. For her remaining years in Paris she shunned them, and was particularly resistant to their efforts to enlist William, her only surviving child (three others had died), into the Irish Legion. They had even gone over her head to the French government, accusing her of keeping William tied to her apron strings. The disputes which Tone had so disliked continued into the Legion; besides, given Napoleon's tendency to treat the Legion as a propaganda tool to scare Britain with groundless threats of invasion, it did not promise the kind of distinguished military career that she sought for her son.

I felt when researching my biography that Tone was increasingly becoming a Frenchman towards the end of his life. He had, after all, served as an officer in its army since 1796. All his life he had wanted to be a soldier and he spoke frequently of his happiness in French uniform. He was also respected by the French officers with whom he operated. Matilda told the Minister for War that 'I never would consent to my son serving as an Emigrant, nor in an emigrant Corps, that his choice and mine was that he should be a Frenchman … and that his Father had paid with all his blood the price of his son's naturalisation'. William trained at the Imperial Cavalry School at St Germain, fought in Napoleon's campaigns of 1813–14 and was awarded the Légion d'Honneur after the Battle of Leipzig. Napoleon thought well of Tone. The day before his suicide in Dublin's Provost prison, Tone wrote a plea to the French Directory to help his family, left destitute in Paris by his loss. It was the personal intervention of the Bonaparte family, including Napoleon himself, that secured Matilda a pension, which continued to be paid until her death. That affinity with France came down through the generations. Kay Dickason spoke French fluently, read French newspapers and holidayed there with her family every year. It was in Paris in 1925 that she married Livingstone T. Dickason, an engineer.

'CHERISH MY MEMORY'
Matilda did follow Tone's last wish to 'cherish my memory', most notably in editing and publishing his *Life* in 1826, thus launching the modern cult of Tone. From America she monitored Irish developments and was annoyed that Tone was not being given his proper place in the national pantheon. She blamed Thomas Moore for not mentioning Tone in his hugely popular *Melodies*, but Daniel O'Connell was her particular villain, for to O'Connell, in his 'moral force' campaign for Catholic Emancipation, the United

Irish tradition was anathema. 'The Liberator does not like us', she complained in December 1842. She welcomed Dr R.R. Madden's *United Irishmen* as 'feeble but honest', even though she thought it 'slovenly written' and was upset that he did not come to see her, as he had visited others among her American-based United Irish friends.

She fervently supported Catholic Emancipation. It is too often forgotten that Tone's most consistent political career in Ireland was as agent and secretary to the Catholic Committee, relying on 'moral force'. O'Connell was of course to be eclipsed by Tone in the development of the militant variety of Irish nationalism in the last century, helped unintentionally by the tailoring of his *Life* by Matilda and son William. Tone was no pacifist, but there is significant evidence that he abhorred indiscriminate killing. 'The great object of my life has been the independence of my country', he said at his trial/court martial in November 1798. 'For a fair and open war I was prepared; if that has degenerated into a system of assassination, massacre, and plunder I do … most sincerely lament it.'

> **'The interest in Tone has never diminished and the arrival of peace in Northern Ireland has allowed us to revisit his life and legacy without the attendant bloodshed so often claimed in his name.'**

My research journey into the United Irishmen and then Tone was undertaken through the worst years of the Northern Ireland Troubles. Working in the archives, with the systems of five different countries and the heightened security in Britain and Ireland, is a story in itself. Militant republicans disliked anyone challenging the image they were presenting of Tone and sent death threats. I am still baffled. They cannot have read the book, which is favourable towards Tone. I already knew Martin Mansergh as a Ph.D student in Oxford and Paris and he asked whether Taoiseach Charles Haughey could launch my book. A head of government launching a book! My publishers at Yale University Press took note and flew in all their main people to Dublin for the Iveagh House event. The Irish consul in New York, Daíthí O Ceallaigh, also gave me a launch. He was criticised by the more republican-leaning Irish-Americans in advance. Again, why? I was an unemployed academic, a bit of a non-entity. I had invited my friends, all the direct descendants of Wolfe Tone, including Kay, and to this day Daithí tells the story of how the republican naysayers were 'astounded'.

The interest in Tone has never diminished and the arrival of peace in Northern Ireland has allowed us to revisit his life and legacy without the attendant bloodshed so often claimed in his name. Once more there is a better understanding of the complexity of this most charismatic historical figure. But I already knew this and cannot but reflect on how much I owed to his descendants, who had preserved his writings through lives that were often tumultuous and uncertain. Although I had the fortune to be the first historian to publish original research findings using the Tone family 'Dickason papers', they are now—at least those of Tone's—in the public domain, thanks to the truly magisterial three-volume *The writings of Theobald Wolfe Tone*, initiated in 1963 by Prof. T.W. Moody and finally brought to fruition by Dr C.J. Woods and Prof. R.B. McDowell between 1998 and 2007.

- *Marianne Elliott is Professor Emerita at the University of Liverpool.*

Below: At the book launch in Iveagh House in 1989 with Taoiseach Charles J. Haughey and my mother. (Yale University Press)

REMEMBERING THE 'FATHER OF IRISH REPUBLICANISM'

BY **GUY BEINER**

IN NOVEMBER 1798, *Walker's Hibernian Magazine* predicted that the name of Wolfe Tone 'will claim a distinguished mention in the history of Ireland'. The arrest of 'the famous Constitution-monger' Theobald Wolfe Tone was reported in Irish newspapers on 27 October 1798, as the battered French flagship *Hoche* was being towed into Lough Swilly—and even before Tone stepped ashore at Buncrana and was infamously spotted by his former Trinity classmate George Hill. The next month, accounts of Tone's trial and death featured in the press, and soon after the *Dublin Evening Post* serialised a biographical sketch of his life. Nevertheless, the *Freeman's Journal* list of 'Memorable Events of the Year 1798', published in January 1799, mentioned these occurrences as just one entry in a particularly eventful year, in which the deluge of news on the rebellion in Ireland competed with other eye-catching items (some of which proved to be misinformation). Although early historical accounts written in the immediate aftermath of the 1798 Rebellion—including even the hostile *Memoirs of the different rebellions in Ireland* by the ultra-loyalist Sir Richard Musgrave—briefly commented on Tone's key role in establishing the United Irishmen, there was little sign that the claim made by *Walker's Hibernian Magazine* would come true.

Above: The *Life of Theobald Wolfe Tone* (Washington DC, 1826), edited by his son William, cemented Tone's reputation as the 'Founder of the United Irish Society' and secured his renown in public memory.

REDISCOVERY

In the following years, when the authorities in Ireland proscribed sympathetic remembrance of the United Irishmen, Wolfe Tone's widow Matilda faithfully preserved the literary remains of her late husband in France and later in America. Matilda Tone's role as custodian of memory was acknowledged by United Irish exiles in 1807, when the Hibernian Provident Society of New York presented her with a medallion (see p. 59), and also awarded her son

Above: The grave of Theobald Wolfe Tone at Bodenstown, 'beautifully rebuilt by Mr Peter Clory of Clane, Co. Kildare', in 1873. The iron railings were added in 1874 to counter the 'pernicious example of carrying off portions of the tomb itself'. (NLI)

William a sword 'with a lively hope that it may one day in his hand avenge the wrongs of his country'. Much to Matilda's chagrin, in 1824 an unauthorised partial 'Auto-Biography' (drawing on a manuscript of 'Memorandums Relative to My Life and Opinions' written in France in late 1796) was serialised in the London *New Monthly Magazine* and then reprinted in Irish newspapers. But it was the publication in Washington DC in 1826 of the two-volume *Life of Theobald Wolfe Tone*, containing diaries, letters and political essays, edited by his son William, and its re-publication by Henry Colburn the next year in London under the title *Memoirs of Theobald Wolfe Tone*, which cemented Tone's reputation as the 'Founder of the United Irish Society' and secured his renown in public memory.

The canonical nineteenth-century biographical history of Tone was written by Richard Robert Madden at a time when the surge of constitutional nationalism led by Daniel O'Connell seemed to have turned its back on Tone's revolutionary radicalism. Madden was reprimanded by 73-year-old Matilda Tone for failing to consult her when writing about her deceased husband in the first series of the first edition of his monumental *The United Irishmen: their lives and times*, published in 1842. This was an uncharacteristic oversight for Madden, who typically made efforts to contact female relatives of executed United Irishmen. He promptly apologised and made amends in an extended memoir published in 1846, which was enhanced with supplementary material in an 1858 revision. Madden concluded that Tone's 'memory is probably destined to survive as long as his country has a history'.

The celebrated writer Thomas Moore was well aware of the revolutionary activities of 'the indefatigable Tone' and consulted his diary as a historical source. Nevertheless, unlike Lord Edward Fitzgerald, who was born and died in the same years as Tone and was eulogised in a biography, or Robert Emmet, who was subtly invoked through an allusion to silent remembrance, the poet chose not to enrol the name of Tone in the pantheon of romantic nationalist memory. This overshadowing of Tone was redressed by Thomas Davis, the leading light of Young Ireland, who was enthused by Madden and became enamoured with 'Wolfe Tone's glorious memoirs'. Even though a projected 'Life of Wolfe Tone' that Davis was determined to write for Young Ireland's Library of Ireland remained incomplete and unpublished on account of his death at an early age from scarlet fever, Davis was responsible more than anyone else for kindling nationalist interest and effectively launching what Marianne Elliott has labelled the 'cult of Tone'.

INITIATING MEMORIALISATION

Through his persistent inquiries, Madden had discovered that Tone was buried in the family plot in Bodenstown churchyard, Co. Kildare. Following this lead, Davis travelled to Bodenstown in the company of John Gray, the proprietor of the *Freeman's Journal*, who recalled in 1873 how a local blacksmith identified the grave site and informed them that 'old and young pay it reverence and while every other grave in the place is walked over, no one walks on that grave; and even the children are taught by the grey-haired men not to harm it, as my father taught me to respect the counsellor's grave'. Returning from this visit, Davis published his poem 'Tone's Grave' in *The Nation* on 25 November 1843, portraying an imaginary gathering of 'students and peasants, the wise and the brave', led by 'an old man who knew him from cradle to grave', who declares: 'we're going to raise him a monument, too—a plain one, yet fit for the simple and true'. In an indication of self-imposed reticence, ellipses mark two absent

> *'old and young pay it reverence and while every other grave in the place is walked over, no one walks on that grave ...'*

stanzas, as if to borrow Moore's mode of silent romanticism. But this was unmistakably a clarion call for commemoration, which was repeatedly reproduced in the many editions of the spin-off anthology *Spirit of the Nation*, and was partly fulfilled when, at the urging of Matilda Tone, Davis commissioned a memorial stone, with Madden among its financers.

The modest commemorative

HISTORY IRELAND/ 87

REMEMBERING THE 'FATHER OF IRISH REPUBLICANISM'

Above: The amalgamated '98 committee of republicans, Parnellites and anti-Parnellites that organised the mass demonstration of 100,000 nationalists in Dublin on 'Wolfe Tone Day' (15 August 1898). Veteran Fenian John O'Leary is seated in the front row (seventh from left).

marker (a fragment of which is now stored at the National Museum of Ireland) was placed on the grave without any publicity, as open commemoration of Tone was apparently still a precarious act. Nonetheless, the devotees of Davis set their sights on defiantly reclaiming the legacy of Tone and the United Irishmen. In the preparations for the failed rising of 1848, a number of Young Ireland confederate clubs were named after Wolfe Tone. At meetings, club members reverently sang John Kells Ingram's poem 'The Memory of the Dead' (first published anonymously in *The Nation* on 1 April 1843), which was popularly known by its stirring opening line, 'Who fears to speak of Ninety-Eight?', urging nationalists to overcome inhibitions and partake in remembrance.

As recalled by the New York Fenian Michael Cavanagh, who participated in a 'pilgrimage to Bodenstown' in 1861 (about which he later reminisced in the 4 July 1898 issue of *Shan Van Vocht*), sporadic visits to Tone's grave by Irish-American Fenians, joined by their counterparts in Ireland, resulted in the 'pernicious example of carrying off portions of the tomb itself'. To counter the damage caused by over-zealous souvenir-hunting, in 1873 a Wolfe Tone Band from Dublin replaced the eroded memorial stone. This time the ceremony was well attended and attracted newspaper coverage. Annual commemorations at the site commenced in 1877.

Tone's standing was meanwhile bolstered by the militant Young Ireland émigré John Mitchel in *The history of Ireland from the Treaty of Limerick* (originally published in 1867), which became a staple of popular nationalist reading. By the end of the nineteenth century Tone's memory was embraced by all shades of nationalism, lauded by Home Rulers like Barry O'Brien (who edited a two-volume autobiography in 1893) as well as radicals like Alice Milligan (who authored a biography in 1898), and in the same centenary year he was even scripted into a melodrama by J.W. Whitbread (see poster on p. 67).

COMMEMORATIVE FERVOUR
Pilgrimages to Bodenstown declined after 1881 only to be revived a decade later, with annual gatherings marking Wolfe Tone's birthday on 20 June initiated in 1891 by Dublin members of a newly founded Young Ireland League, whose motivation to engage in commemoration was invigorated by the memorialisation of Charles Stewart Parnell. Despite the grave being protected since 1874 by iron railings erected by the 'Men of Co. Kildare', the chipping away of fragments continued. In 1895 the memorial was once again replaced, this time by the local Kildare Gaelic Athletic Association, together with a Fenian-affiliated National Monuments Committee. Commemoration of Tone reached its zenith in 1898 during the centenary of the 1798 rebellion, which saw numerous events honouring the memory of the United Irishmen throughout Ireland and Irish diaspora communities.

Having squandered many months on factional infighting, it was only in June 1898, after a particularly large attendance at the annual commemoration in Bodenstown, that the various competing organisations of Irish nationalism managed to put aside their internecine rivalries and cooperate constructively in planning the centenary's main event. An amalgamated '98 committee brought republicans together with represen-

Below: The foundation stone of the Wolfe Tone monument, laid by John O'Leary on 15 August 1898 at St Stephen's Green (where the Fusiliers' Arch, a.k.a. 'Traitors' Gate', now stands). In *Ulysses* James Joyce referred to it as 'the slab where Wolfe Tone's statue was not'. Today it sits in Croppies Acre. (Donal Fallon)

tatives of both the Parnellite and anti-Parnellite wings of the Irish Parliamentary Party at a public meeting in Dublin with the purpose, as reported in the *Freeman's Journal* (21 June 1898), 'of taking steps toward perpetuating the name of Theobald Wolfe Tone, by the erection in the city of a public memorial'.

On 15 August 1898, Lady Day (the Catholic Feast of the Assumption of the Virgin Mary) was redesignated 'Wolfe Tone Day' in a mass demonstration of 100,000 nationalists, who paraded through the streets of Dublin and assembled at the north-west corner of St Stephen's Green to watch the veteran Fenian John O'Leary lay a foundation stone for a monument, using a ceremonial trowel sent from America by Tone's granddaughter. The stone, which had been transported from Belfast with much pomp, was hewn from McArt's Fort on Cave Hill, where in 1795 Tone and a core group of United Irishmen had taken a 'solemn obligation … never to desist in our efforts, until we have subverted the authority of England over our country and asserted her independence'. This high-profile nationalist celebration, which was widely publicised in the press, antagonised loyalists in Ulster, who attacked the trains of the northern participants on their return from Dublin, sparking violent riots that pitted—as depicted in the contrasting headlines of nationalist and unionist newspapers—'Orange rowdies' against 'Toners and Stoners'. This outburst was an early forewarning of Ulster loyalist predisposition to 'decommemorating', which would return with a vengeance later in the twentieth century.

MEMORIALISATION *IN ABSENTIA*

In spite of all the enthusiasm, commemoration in Dublin did not ultimately go according to plan. The design for the intended Wolfe Tone monument was selected by competition, but the chosen proposal by the Manchester-based Irish sculptor John Cassidy for an impressive centennial monument, which was on a scale of grandeur that would have matched Dublin's O'Connell monument, never materialised. Insufficient fund-raising incurred prolonged delays. James Joyce—a perceptive witness to these setbacks—showed little sentimentality for the unfulfilled commemoration, portraying in *A portrait of the artist as a young man* a scene in which Stephen Daedalus passes the site where 'a slab was set to the memory of Wolfe Tone' and recalls 'having been present with his father at its laying', while noting that 'he remembered with bitterness that scene of tawdry tribute'. In *Ulysses* (set in 1904), Joyce again mentioned the place, this time even more sardonically, as 'the slab where Wolfe Tone's statue was not'. Nationalist incompetence left the space vacant to be claimed by unionists, and in 1907 the Fusiliers' Arch—a monument to Irish soldiers who died in imperial service during the Boer War—was unveiled on the site (the foundation stone from 1898 was later removed by the Board of Works and is now in Croppies Acre).

The depletion of the funds of the Wolfe Tone Memorial Committee, partly a result of embezzlement, led to a hiatus in commemoration at Bodenstown between 1906 and 1910, which ended when Thomas Clarke (who during his time in New York had made annual pilgrimages to the grave of Matilda Tone in Brooklyn's Greenwood cemetery) revived the annual commemorations. Clarke and his fellow conspirators in the IRB used these memorial gatherings—which somehow passed below the radar of the intelligence services—to stage revolutionary rallies of militant separatists, who found inspiration in Tone's dictum 'to subvert the tyranny of our execrable Government, to break the connection with England, the never-failing source of all our political evils, and to assert the independence of my country'.

Patrick Pearse delivered the speech on 22 June 1913, proclaiming Bodenstown 'the holiest place in Ireland' and heaping on Tone a string of superlatives: 'the greatest of all that have died for Ireland whether in old time or in new'; 'the greatest of Irish Nationalists'; 'the greatest of

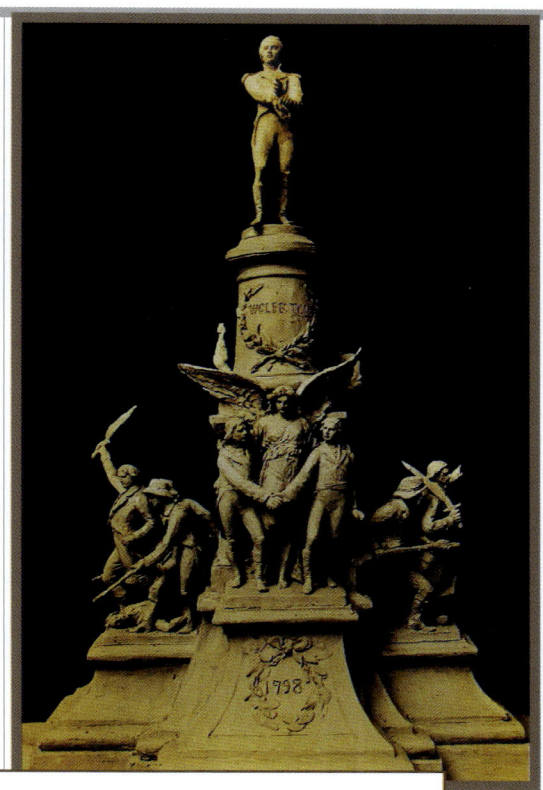

Above: A macquette of Manchester-based Irish sculptor John Cassidy's centennial monument, which was on a scale of grandeur that would have matched Dublin's O'Connell monument—it never materialised. (Peter Davis/Manchester Academy of Fine Arts)

Irish men'; 'the greatest of our dead'; 'one of the great implacable exiles of Irish history'; and 'the greatest of the men of '98'. Pearse maintained that Tone's writings formulated 'the gospel of Irish Nationalism', hence 'we owe to this dead man more than we can ever repay him by making pilgrimages to his grave or by rearing to him the stateliest monument in the streets of his city'. In the build-up towards the Easter Rising, the memory of Wolfe Tone had evidently reached its apotheosis.

RIVAL COMMEMORATIONS

Following the Irish revolution and Civil War, Bodenstown became an arena for competition between rival factions, each claiming to best represent the republican ideal. Whereas the Irish Free State assigned the commemoration to the Defence Forces, the official ceremonies were challenged by alternative commemorations organised by the IRA and Sinn Féin, as well as by Fianna Fáil (which

REMEMBERING THE 'FATHER OF IRISH REPUBLICANISM'

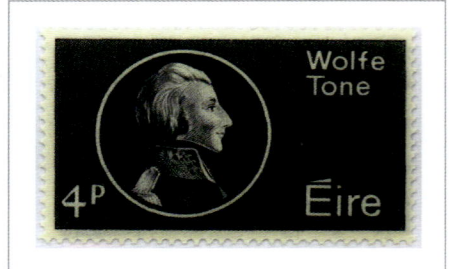

continued whether the party was in opposition or in government). From the 1940s, the National Graves Association (closely aligned with the republican movement) assumed on its own accord responsibility for maintenance of the site and, despite the hostility between those attending the competing commemorations, displays of violence were relatively scarce.

While Tone was widely recognised as a national hero, his radicalism posed difficulties for newly independent Ireland's conservative Catholic culture. In a biography written in 1935, Aodh de Blacam attempted to resolve the conflict by portraying Tone as 'one of the founders of modern Catholic Democracy'. By contrast, the devout Jesuit writer Leo McCabe (Denis Peter Fennell SJ) denounced Tone as an anti-Catholic 'shameless hypocrite and selfish adventurer'. The *Wolfe Tone Weekly*, founded in 1937 by the republican activists Brian O'Higgins and Joseph Clarke, was suppressed by the authorities in September 1939, yet O'Higgins continued to publish the *Wolfe Tone Annual*, which was founded in 1932 for the purpose of raising funds for commemorating Tone.

Sustained popular interest is manifest in the many biographies and reissues of his diaries. Seán O'Faolain, in his abridged *Autobiography of Theobald Wolfe Tone* (1937), suggested that the realist appeal of Tone's writings had 'deprived him of the romantic Irishman's final mark of respect—he has no statue'. Commemorative stamps honouring Tone were issued in 1948 (the sesquicentenary of the 1798 rebellion) and in 1964 (the bicentenary of his birth, albeit a year late), but the continuing absence of a fitting monument in the capital was a cause of enduring frustration.

Faithful to her husband's legacy after his execution in 1916, Kathleen Clarke stayed on for decades as trustee of the Wolfe Tone Memorial Fund, which over the years benefited from donations accumulated through countless sporting matches, concerts, raffles and subscriptions, and repeatedly petitioned the government for supplementary funding. This long saga of persistent commemorative devotion finally came to fruition after a Wolfe Tone Memorial Competition held in 1964 brought about the unveiling by President Eamon de Valera in 1967 of a statue by sculptor Edward Delaney, which was placed by the architect Noel Keating at the north-eastern corner of St Stephen's Green in front of a row of granite monoliths (almost immediately nicknamed 'Tonehenge'). In a poem written in 1957 in response to the destruction by the IRA of the monument to Viscount Gough in the Phoenix Park, Austin Clarke had reflected on the memory of Wolfe Tone, wryly observing that 'we cannot blow his statue up'. A decade later this was no longer the case.

Below: Edward Delaney's 'Tonehenge', unveiled by President Eamon de Valera in 1967. It was blown up by loyalist paramilitaries on 8 February 1971 in an act of 'decommemoration'.

TROUBLES WITH TONE

Politicised remembrance of Tone was implicated in the radicalisation of republicanism, which commenced sometime before the 50th jubilee of the Easter Rising. Wolfe Tone Directories established by republicans in 1963 to commemorate the bicentenary of his birth were superseded the following year by a Wolfe Tone Society, which initiated a series of discussions that brought about the establishment in 1967 of the Northern Ireland Civil Rights Association (NICRA), kick-starting the northern civil rights movement. With the turn towards armed struggle, the IRA co-opted the memory of Wolfe Tone and the United Irishmen in its rhetoric and symbolism. Mirroring the split in Sinn Féin, from 1970 the Officials ('Stickies') and the Provisionals (Provos) held separate annual commemorations at Bodenstown. This would not pass unnoticed by loyalist paramilitaries, who embarked on a cycle of violent decommemoration that targeted remembrance of Tone in the South.

On 30 October 1969, the UVF detonated an explosion at Bodenstown that destroyed the memorial of 'the traitor Wolfe Tone'. Extensive renovation undertaken by the National Graves Association levelled the historical grave site and constructed in 1971 a designated platform for political rallies. That same year, the UVF struck again on 8 February, blowing to pieces the Delaney statue in Dublin, which required extensive restoration. Apprehensive of paramilitary involvement at Bodenstown, in 1973 the Irish government withdrew the Defence Forces from the commemorations. In turn, the Irish Republican Socialist Party (IRSP)—the political wing of the Irish National Liberation Army (INLA)—added in 1975 its own demonstrations at Bodenstown, competing with the other republican commemorations. That year a failed loyalist terrorist attack targeted a train carrying passengers travelling to Bodenstown. There were those amongst the general public who felt growing unease with the memory of Tone, which became less appealing through its association with the violence of the Troubles. Commemoration remained on a low flame until the bicentenary of 1798 in 1998, which coincided with the brokering of the Good Friday Agreement and the end of the Troubles.

REPUBLICAN FATHERHOOD

With the history of Tone's memory in mind, it is instructive to consider when he became the 'father of Irish republicanism'. In his own lifetime, the loyalist Earl of Clare, John Fitzgibbon, labelled Tone the 'father of the Society of United Irishmen', which is not quite the same. Neither Madden nor Davis, who were largely responsible for the rediscovery of Tone's memory in the 1840s, referred to him as a father of republicanism. The highly influential publication *Speeches from the dock*, which was authored by the Sullivan brothers in 1867 and was reissued in multiple editions—effectively defining the canon of nationalist-republican martyrdom—referred to Tone as the national movement's 'main-spring—its leading spirit'. Speaking in 1874 at the Catholic Institute in Edinburgh on the topic of 'The Martyrs of Irish Liberty', the former Fenian and early Home Ruler John O'Connor Power mentioned that Tone 'might properly be called the father of Irish Republicanism' in what may be one of the earliest evocations of this formula, which was not widely repeated. Even Pearse in his hyperbolic 1913 graveside panegyric at Bodenstown did not explicitly refer to Tone as a father-figure.

Unlike biological fathers who beget children, national father-figures are often retrospective constructions or—to use a term coined by the historian Eric Hobsbawm—'invented traditions'. The appellation 'father of Irish republicanism' was apparently introduced in the years after independence, only gaining currency from the 1930s onwards. In other words, it was the generation of his great-great-grandchildren that would bestow this recognition on Tone, creating an imagined retroactive genealogy. In subsequent decades this reference would become an oft-repeated cliché, giving the impression that it had always been in existence. And yet, despite established practices of com-

> **' ... the memory of Wolfe Tone—and with it the radical legacy of late eighteenth-century republicanism—still bides its time ... '**

memoration, Tone's memory remains unstable. The 250th anniversary of his birth in 2013 was overshadowed by the commemorative programme of the Decade of Centenaries, and the 225th anniversary of his death in 2023 was eclipsed by the 25th anniversary of the Good Friday Agreement, so that both dates passed without garnering widespread public attention. Rather than simply declining over time, remembrance waxes and wanes, with recurring moments of commemorative regeneration countering lapses of oblivious neglect. It would seem that, having had its ebbs and flows, the memory of Wolfe Tone—and with it the radical legacy of late eighteenth-century republicanism—still bides its time, waiting to land once more upon Ireland's shores.

- *Guy Beiner is the Sullivan Chair in Irish Studies at Boston College.*

FURTHER READING

P. Collins, *Who fears to speak of '98? Commemoration and the continuing impact of the United Irishmen* (Belfast, 2004).

C. Kennedy, 'Republican relicts: gender, memory, and mourning in Irish nationalist culture, c. 1798–1848', *Journal of British Studies* **59** (3) (2020), 608–37.

J. Quinn, 'Theobald Wolfe Tone and the historians', *Irish Historical Studies* **32** (125) (2000), 113–28.

C.J. Woods, *Bodenstown revisited: the grave of Theobald Wolfe Tone, its monuments and its pilgrimages* (Dublin, 2018).

AFTERWORD
WHAT WOULD TONE DO?

BY **BILL ATKINS**

'Ireland [was] founded on the old French and United Ireland republican values of equality and liberty'—President Michael D. Higgins.

In Ireland today we see parallels to an American cultural experience that has led to a resurgence of virulent forms of nationalist populism designed to harness the sentiments of those who feel marginalised by 'the system'. How would Tone have responded?

The United Irish diaspora of the late 1790s caused a harsh reaction in America from the more extreme Federalists. Rufus King, the US minister in London, had the ear of Secretary of State Thomas Pickering, who in 1798 ordered 'that descriptive criteria be drawn up to ensure that "United Irish Desperadoes" would not be able to enter the United States'. This was the transatlantic political theatre in full production, seeking to brand the United Irish as pernicious agents of change and even chaos. It was three years later, in 1802, after Jefferson became president, that Thomas Addis Emmet, William Sampson, William James MacNevin, Robert Adrian and Thomas O'Connor were permitted entry.

Immigration is not a new bogeyman, but a more evolved form of Irish chauvinism could metastasise from the current socio-political milieu if not faced head-on. Opponents of immigration aggressively embrace the 'other' narrative by branding immigrants felonious, infectious and dilutive of national populist norms. Tone resolutely believed that the rights of man and citizenship were universal. His communication skills and humanity allowed him to convince non-Catholics that priestcraft and Catholic superstition were 'fake news'. We have to believe that he would make short work of today's racists by exposing their inhumanity, but also by appealing to the concerns of their followers about marginalisation. Who better than Tone to debate the greater good for the greater number?

Nevertheless, the head winds are significant. In 2019 Danish political scientist Michael Bang Petersen studied why people share conspiracy theories that they know to be false. He measured the need for chaos in a representative sample of Americans and found that 30% *did not* reject the statement 'I think society should be burned to the ground'. He discovered that it was due primarily to a perceived rise in inequality, which they blame on élites in politics, the media and the boardroom. Researchers found that 'the root cause of the need for chaos is the clash between status aspirations and thwarted opportunities'. Having a pervasive feeling of being stuck, these people feel that their only recourse to combat societal marginalisation is to mess it up. Tone would certainly empathise with this cohort by agreeing about numerous present-day élite failures in public health, national media and housing, to name but a few. He would then deconstruct their information pipeline and cull out a sampling of false and misleading sources for rigorous debate.

Ireland is not alone as it tries to manage the massive influx of refugees and immigrants from different countries and cultures. The global displacement of people is increasing owing to war, sectarian conflict, famine, natural disasters and the effects of climate change. Tone would be the first to point out that these people are a resource, not a burden, and that Ireland has the opportunity to lead an Atlantic coalition of nations willing to face this crisis. The proper assimilation of foreign nationals serves many needs not addressed by the native population. This includes a way to respond to an expanding tourism market and international economic opportunities.

Ironically, a way for the marginalised to get unstuck is to recognise that these immigrants will eventually be able to fill their dead-end jobs, rent their miserable flats and buy their rusted-out, high-mileage vehicles. Then it will be up to the 'stuck' to discover the abundance mentality that Tone so ably represented when he sought a common name for Irishman that would include Protestant, Catholic and Dissenter. *Nil desperandum!*

● Bill Atkins is a direct descendent of Thomas Tone, great-uncle of Theobald Wolfe Tone, whose son John Tone emigrated to America in 1740.

Above: 'The Unfortunate Theobald Wolfe Tone, esq' as depicted in his French uniform following his capture in October 1798. (*Walker's Hibernian Magazine*)